A Handbook
Cornish Surnames

Compiled by
G.Pawley White
(Gunwyn)
Past Grand Bard, Gorseth Kernow

Dhe Gof
Den a Growan

DYLLANSOW TRURAN

First published in 1972

Second Edition 1981
Published by Dyllansow Truran

Third edition 1999
Dyllansow Truran
Croft Prince, Mount Hawke, Truro TR4 8EE

ISBN 1 85022 127 8

Design by Ray Lancefield
ray@thedesignfield.com

Printed in Cornwall by R.Booth (Bookbinder) Ltd
& Troutbeck Press Antron Hill, Mabe, Penryn, TR10 9HH

Main text set in Goudy 11/12pt

INTRODUCTION

An urgent request from Dr. A. L. Rowse for a book of Cornish Surnames led to the preparation of this survey. In the course of his travels in the United States of America, Dr. Rowse had been fascinated by his discovery of the part which Cornish people played in the building up of that new nation, and this resulted in his writing of 'The Cornish in America'. John Spargo, William Prowse, William Treloar, Charles Vivian, the Penrose family and a host of others with distinctively Cornish surnames are mentioned in that book as pioneers who markedly influence the development of the new communities in America. Many of their present-day descendants have none but the most tenuous links with their ancestors' homeland, but their names give evidence of their Cornish descent. In view of the great interest shown in their names by many of the folk whom he met, Dr. Rowse, in an appendix to his book, suggested the meanings of some 250 of them. The present work aims at amplifying the list, which he compiled.

Fortunate, indeed, it was that at the time of Dr. Rowse's request, that veteran Cornish scholar, the late Mr. R. R. Blewett of St. Day, had completed his enormous task of analysing the 1953 Electoral Registers for the five Cornish Parliamentary Divisions, which he had commenced in 1954, at the age of 73. He extracted the surnames of all the 243,389 voters, so that he could know the number of people bearing each surname, and the parish or town in which they lived. Thus he ascertained their distribution in the County and the places of their concentration. Having analysed the information, he then searched for the surnames of Celtic origin. Realising that many were associated with Cornish place names, he began an extended study of 'The Place Names of Cornwall', a collection of some 10,000 names with attempted explanations of their etymology by J. E. Gover (1928) in the Royal Institution of Cornwall. Then, with the help of Dictionaries, he began to unravel their meanings, and, in 1970, completed his work entitled 'Celtic Surnames in Cornwall, Their Distribution and Population in 1953, Their Origins, History and Etymology' in two volumes, as yet unpublished. When I requested his help he most generously allowed me to have his manuscript, and to make of it whatever use I wished. Without the benefit of all his research on the subject, I doubt if this book would ever have been compiled. I would like to acknowledge the inestimable help and encouragement, which I received from him.

G. Pawley White
May 1972

PREFACE TO THE THIRD EDITION

Since this book first saw the light in 1972, copies have found their way all over the world, and appear to have strengthened the links between the dispersed Cornish communities and their Homeland of Kernow. This new edition incorporates the Appendix of the Second edition and some new material that has cropped up since then. It has been thought advisable to omit the Non-Celtic Surnames, and those of biblical characters and of Kings and Heroes. Some of the surnames listed as no longer being in use in Cornwall have since been discovered in our midst and many more are found overseas. Some additions have been made to the Bibliography.

Many changes have occurred during the 27 years of the book's existence. Dr. A.L. Rowse, whose urgency and encouragement led to its origin has died – a great loss to Cornish scholarship. Len Truran, the original publisher (Dyllansow Truran) has also passed from us, after having made a worthy contribution to Cornish publishing.

I have been gratified to meet readers of the book in Australia, New Zealand, South Africa, Canada and the USA and am humbly grateful that they have found it of use and interest. I trust that my new readers will be pleased as this new edition makes its way into the world.

Pawley White 1999

FOREWORD

Many people have been struck by the individuality, to them the strangeness, sometimes the beauty of Cornish names – and this goes for surnames as well as those of the places from which they often come. There is the old rhyme, known to Walter Scott:

By Tre-, Pol-, Pen-,
Ye may know most Cornish men.

That is to say, such names as Tremayne, Polglase, Penrose. The first line sometimes goes:

By Ros-, Car-, Lan-, Tre-, Pol-, Pen-,

to give us such names as Roskelly or Rosevear, Carlyon or Cardew, Lander or Lanyon. Altogether, I fancy there is evidence of perhaps a thousand specific Cornish names – some of the most famous of which seem to have died out, like Killigrew and Carminow, others on the way to dying out, like Godolphin; while one solitary bird of the name Pencover survived up to recently.

But what do these names mean? That is the question; and there must be many people who would like to know the answers.

First, those who have a Cornish surname – I never knew the meaning of mine until this useful book told me. We all want to know what our names mean. There are Cornish folk all over the world who would like to know. Then there are hundreds of thousands of visitors to Cornwall every year, many of whom are curious about our characteristics and ways different from other peoples' – are interested in our history, the villages and country places which have given surnames to our folk. There are the other Celtic peoples, who are akin to us, and English-speaking peoples at home and abroad who may be glad to be enlightened.

The greatest of English writers, Shakespeare, thought Leroy a Cornish name; but he was wrong.

It is not an easy subject; indeed I found it very provoking not to be able to make out the meanings of a large number Cornish surnames, when I was writing my book on The Cornish in America. I only wish I had had Mr. Pawley White's Guide to them to help me. Now he has come to the aid of us all, and we have reason to be grateful.

All sorts of things can happen through not knowing the proper meaning of our names. I have heard of a family in Australia, of the good old Cornish name of Bosanko, who thought they must be Italian. A well-known American historian told me he always thought that John Spargo – famous Socialist leader and writer in his day – was a Russian! Then there are those who think Santo, Jago, Clemo etc. must be survivors of the Spanish Armada! (No ship of the Armada came ashore on the Cornish coast).

I once heard a story of a Baragwanath in South Africa during the Boer War, whom the British Army arrested and detained as an alien on account of his name, thinking him a Boer. They paid a tidy little sum in compensation when they found out the truth.

So you see there are disadvantages attached to not recognising our names.

Again, people will deform their names on account of ignorance. A well-known footballer imparted to the press the information that his name Trebilcock was originally Trebilco – nonsense, of course: he wouldn't know. I have come across all sorts of deformations of our names in America: Pellymounter had become Palamountain, Chenoweth (properly pronounced Shenóweth) had become Chenworth and Chinworth, because they didn't know what it meant. Uren was made ridiculous as U'Ren, because they didn't know how to pronounce either Uren or urine they thought it sounded like. Or again people will uglify their name and make themselves look silly by playing tricks with it, cutting the poor thing in two, like Pen-Gilly.

You see how much we need to know about our names: we should stick to their proper forms and get them right. Here this little book comes in handy, and is indispensable.

Many of our names are beautiful, some of them poetic. Though this book assures me that my name is Cornish, it might be mistaken for an English Rouse – how much nicer to have one recognisable at once, like Nancarrow or Trevorrow, Nankivell or Trevanion; Carlyon, Pendarves, Penhallow; Colenso, Carnsew, Polglaze, Trevelyan, Tregarthen; Bonython, Vellanoweth, Andrewartha. I would swop my name any day for one of those.

Some of the most beautiful of our names are rare and dying out. There are all too many Browns, Smiths and Joneses. I suggest that we keep up our Cornishry by using some of these as second names, e.g. if you are a Brown, what about John Rosevear Brown, or Mark Trevanion Smith? Quite a number of English people mark a line of Cornish descent this way.

Then there is the question of accent and pronunciation. In Cornish names the accent comes usually, though not always on the second syllable; so the proper pronunciation is Penróse, Rosevéar or Rosewárne, Restárick, Chenóweth. In England and America the tendency is to shift the accent to the front, so we get Pénrose; the America Restáricks and Chenóweths call themselves Réstaricks and Chénoweths, which is not only wrong but hard to say. On the other hand they keep the proper pronunciation of Trevelyan by spelling it Trevillian – there are hundreds of them in America, very few left in Cornwall.

I cannot here go into what vistas of history these names familiar to us, strange to others, open up – though through these names we can tell at a glance something of the contribution the Cornish folk have made to other peoples. If it is English history there is the work of the great translator John C Trevisa, alongside of Wycliffe; Lord Godolphin, Queen Anne's Prime Minister who brought about the Act of Union with Scotland and presided over affairs at home while Marlborough fought France abroad;

or spirited Admiral Boscawen, or any number of gay Killigrews; or John Opie, Richard Trevithick or Humphrey Davy.

If it is America we have Chief Justice Penhallow in early New Hampshire; a number of Penroses, including a famous Senator, and the leading Mormon hymn-writer; the Mormon Temple at Salt Lake City was built mostly by a Moyle; the creator of that very American institution, the Order of Elks, was a Vivian. The foremost American anthropologist today is a Coon. If only we had had a Tre-, Pol-, or Pen-, as President!

In South Africa there is noble Bishop Colenso, pioneer of commonsense about the Bible and defender of the blacks. In East Africa there was the great Baptist missionary, a Grenfell; in West Africa, a Lander discovered the sources of the Niger.

In India a Cornish Sleeman suppressed the murderous institution of Thuggee. (The Indians have reason to be grateful). In New Zealand, there is another Colenso, first of their naturalists; today their leading poet is a Curnow. In Australia there are Field-Marshal Blamey, first of her soldiers, or the philanthropic Bonythons. In Canada a Grenfell was the great missionary doctor of Labrador; a Yeo founded the colony of Prince Edward Island.

All these have recognisable Cornish names. But, as this book tells us, unfortunately it is only a minority of us who have these distinctive names. The majority of us have English names like Brown, Smith, Jones, Williams, Harris, Thomas – we might as well come from Birmingham or Clapham. (What about changing into Cornish names, and reviving some of the rare ones? I have sometimes written, in America, under the name Trenarren).

At any rate, here at last we have a guide to tell us what our names mean, and I for one have learned a lot of things I didn't know from Mr. Pawley White's valuable book. There are still things we do not know, uncertainties to clear up and knotty points for people to untie. But I hope this book will start something with Cornish folk all over the world, and be of use to all English-speaking people who want to know more about us both at home and abroad.

A. L. Rowse

CORNISH SURNAMES

It was not until the early Middle Ages that surnames were first used to distinguish between numbers of people bearing the same personal, or Christian, name. With the growth of documentation in the later Middle Ages, such names became essential, and a person whose distinguishing name described his trade, his place of residence, his father's name, or some personal characteristic, passed that name on to his children and the surname became hereditary.

Naturally, the spelling of such surnames varied according to the clerk who inscribed them on documents, and over succeeding generations a name might be altered out of all recognition through a series of mis-spellings by those who were only semi-literate. It was not until centuries later that spelling became anything like standardised, and, in fact, it was only with the appearance of Samuel Johnson's Dictionary in the mid 18th century that the spelling of English was acceptably fixed.

This being the case with a living, written and developing language like English, how much more difficult it was to approach a standardised spelling in Cornish, which had no great literary corpus, which had been in decline from the 15th century onwards, and which had few traditional spellings. It is necessary to refer to the oldest form of spelling available in order to obtain some clue as to the origin of a name. The Lay Subsidy Rolls of 1327 and 1523, together with the Parish Registers from 1600 –1812, afford a great deal of light on the spelling and location of names. In the course of his work, Mr R. R. Blewett made very considerable use of these sources.

Cornish surnames fall roughly into five main classes.

1. PATRONYMICS

(a) The father's name is taken and used as a surname without alteration, e.g. Davy, Harry.
(b) A diminutive of the father's name is used, e.g. Jenkin, Hockin.
(c) A Christian name, or its diminutive, is used with an English possessive 's' suffixed, e.g. Johns, Roberts, Jenkins, Rogers.
(d) The prefix Map (son of) or its residual 'p' is attached to the father's name, e.g. Map Robert becomes Probert, Map Rowse becomes Prowse, Map Howell becomes Powell.

2. NAMES FROM PLACES OF RESIDENCE

These are the most prolific of Cornish surnames. The well-known prefixes of CAR or KER (fort or camp), TRE (homestead), POL (pool), PEN (head or end), ROS (heath or promontory), LAN (enclosure, sometimes monastic), BOS (dwelling) and many others are used to form place names in conjunction with a personal name, an adjective or other distinctive feature.

e.g.   CARDEW : car-du, black or dark camp
POLMEAR : pol – mur, big pool
TRESKEWES : tre-skewys, sheltered homestead
PENGELLY : pen- (k)gelly, end of copse
ROSEVEAR : ros- (ṁ)vur, great heath
LANDRY : lan- (t)dre, churchyard or glebe
BOSCAWEN : bos-scawen, dwelling by elder trees

(It should be noted that the Celtic system of mutation of initial letters under certain conditions applies. Hence in the foregoing 'm' has become 'v' and 't' has become 'd'.)

3. NAMES TAKEN FROM OCCUPATIONS

A few names are taken from occupations, all to do with the primary occupations of the community, e.g.

DYER: tyor; thatcher
LAITY: leth – ty; milk-house, hence dairyman
TRAHAIR: tregher; cutter, tailor
MARRACK : marghek; rider, or knight
ANGOVE: an-gof; the smith
HELLYER: helghyer; hunter

4. NICKNAMES OR NAMES DERIVED FROM PERSONAL CHARACTERISTICS

For example:
LEGASSICK :lagasek; big-eyed
PENNECK : pennek; big-headed
COATH,COAD : coth; old
COUCH : cough; red
DOWLING : deulyn; knees
TALLACK : talek; big browed
CUNNACK : connek; clever, cunning
ANGWIN : an gwyn; the white or fair one (perhaps a miller)

5. NAMES TAKEN FROM ANIMALS

There are few of these, e.g.
BLIGH,BLEE : blyth: wolf, BATH : bath: boar,
LEWARNE : lowarn: fox, BROCK : brogh: badger

It is sometimes thought that a number of the 'Spanish looking' names borne by Cornish people are derived from supposed survivors from Armada wrecks of 1588, (there were none on the Cornish coast), or from the brief Spanish incursion into Mount's Bay in 1595. There is no justification for this theory, as names such as Clemo (recorded in the 14th Century), Bennetto (recorded in 1546) and Jose (1523), were already in use in Cornwall before this time, and the derivation of such names as Tregenza, Santo and Bosanko can easily be traced to Cornish origins. Many of the Cornish surnames ending in 'o' or 'ow' show an ancient plural or adjectival ending, e.g. Pasco (Easter children), Crebo (crests, ridges), or are added to shortened familiar names to indicate 'children of', e.g. Clemo, Clemmow (Clement's children) Bennetto (Benedict's children), Kittow (Christopher's children). Another frequent ending is 'y' suffixed to shortened Christian names, similarly to indicate 'kin of' e.g. Eddy, Harry, Davy, Pawley.

Possibly many of the names here included as Cornish may be of other origin. Successive waves of incomers, Irish, Welsh, Breton, Scots, English, French, have been assimilated into the Cornish community, and their names have become so respelt as to be unrecognisable, or some have adopted Cornish forms of their names. Conversely, some Cornish names were translated into English as, for example, Angwyn has become the English 'White'. In addition, as Nance says 'there are even a few non-Celtic personal names that are old enough to come into place names beginning with Tre-, besides many more in present use that have been so long in Cornwall that they have become 'typically Cornish'. Some of those who bear Saxon names may indeed be now more Celtic than many who carry a fine old Cornish Tre- name. For it must be allowed that the most aristocratic of Cornish surnames may record only the looting, by a Norman, of the estate of a Saxon, who dispossessed the heir of a Cornishman, who founded it and gave it his own name with Tre- before it; while the Cornish founder's heirs may still walk among us bearing, perhaps, like so many Celts in Wales some name such as Williams, Thomas or Richards, that tells nothing of their long Celtic heritage'.[1]

However, it is certain that the names listed herein as Celtic Cornish were all borne by inhabitants of Cornwall in the year 1953. The interpretation of those names is likely to continue to be a matter for argument or discussion, but this careful listing by Mr. H. H. Blewett of the names does provide for the first time a solid basis from which to work. As Jenner says of place names 'the interpretation is not so simple as it looks, and it is easier to criticise other people's derivations than to find better ones'.[2]

1.   R. Morton Nance: Celtic Personal Names of Cornwall.
      (Old Cornwall, Vol. iv, No. 2, p.68).
2.   Henry Jenner: A Handbook of the Cornish Language p.202.

NAMES OF CELTIC ORIGIN WITH DERIVATIONS, AREAS OF CONCENTRATION IN 1953 AND RELEVANT PLACE NAMES

Abell, Abel, Able	From a-bell: far off. Or possibly Biblical name Abel. Now found mostly in SE. Cornwall.
Ahearn	From hern, plural of horn: iron. Probably of Irish origin. Now found mostly in Bodmin-Padstow area.
Allen	From personal name Allen (Bret), Alun (W). Parish name: St. Allen.
Allett	From place name Allett, Kenwyn parish. Known as Aled 1284, Alet 1209.
Ancell, Ansell	From an seghla: the dry place. Place name Zelah, St. Allen. Widely scattered.
Andain, Andean, Endean	From an den: the man (probably a leading man). Found mostly in St. Agnes, Penryn and Saltash.
Andrewartha	From an dre wartha: the upper homestead. Place name Trewartha. Concentrated in SW. Cornwall.
Angear	From an ger: the fort, earthwork or camp. Place name Gear in St. Ewe, St. Erth and Camborne parishes inter alia. See also Gear, Tregear and Care.
Angell	From an gell: the light brown, tawny. Name found in 16th-18th cents. in 9 parishes. Pronounced with hard 'g'.
Angilley	From an (k)gelly: the grove. Known in St. Austell area for 7 centuries. Place name in St. Dennis and St. Stephen-in-Brannel parishes.
Angove	From an gof: the smith. Concentrated from 14th cent. onwards West of Truro.
Angrave	From an gravyor: the sculptor, carver. Place name found in St. Breward and Newquay parishes. Alternative derivation: An (c) gref: the strong one.
Angwin	From an gwyn: the white or fair (man). Found mostly in West Cornwall. Chirgwin suggests alternative derivation from Angevin (F): refugee from Anjou or Angers.

Annan, Anning	Personal name, found in place name Bodannan (Bod-Annan, dwelling of Annan), St. Breock.
Annear	From an hyr: the long or tall (man). Mostly in Mid-Cornwall. See Mennear, Manhire, Hare.
Annis, Anniss	Still extant in Plymouth areas. Possibly from enys: island or isolated place.
Anstey	Still found in Plymouth and Falmouth areas. See Anstice. In 1327 Thos. Anstros lived in St. Austell. Possibly from stros: the low ground.
Anstice, Anstiss, Enstice	Name found mostly in Mid-Cornwall. Origin obscure. Possibly from An-ys-ty: the under house.
Argall	From argel: retreat, shelter. Place name Argall, Budock parish, recorded in 1327. Now found in Truro, Redruth, Feock area.
Arscott	Possibly from Breton, harscoet: iron shield.
Arthur	Possibly from arth-wr: bear man. Personal name. Found throughout Cornwall. Place name Carnarthen (formerly Carnarther) Illogan parish.
Bain, Bane, Bean	First two Scottish forms of 'little' and third Cornish byhan: little. Recorded in early 16th cent. in Camborne. Now in small groups from E. to W Cornwall.
Baragwanath, Baragwaneth	From bara gwaneth: wheaten bread. Name mentioned in 16th cent. in Towednack parish. Now widely scattered throughout Cornwall.
Barfett	Name mentioned in Domesday Book. Probably from Trebarfoot, Poundstock. Perveth: middle, interior.
Barnicoat, Barnecutt	Possibly from bar an cos: top of the wood.
Bassett	Chirgwin suggests from bassya: become lower or shallow, hence of short stature.
Bastian	Shortened form of Sebastian.
Bath	From bath: boar, or possibly from bagh: nook, corner, place where streams, ridges or tracks meet. Sometimes found as Bach, Bache, Bagg, Back.

Beaglehole	From bugel hal: herdsman of the moor.
Bedell, Bodell, Beadell, Biddle	Originally Bod Dell: dwelling of Dell (personal name).
Behenna	Either from Bod Hennah: dwelling of Hannah, or late comparative of byghan-byghenna: smaller.
Beith	Possibly 2nd element of place name, Trebeath, Egloskerry, and likely to be personal name, or of Scottish origin.
Bell	From a-bell: far off, distant dweller. Mostly in West Cornwall.
Benallack, Bonallack	From benalek: broom-brake. Place names in Probus, St. Enoder, Constantine and Mabe parishes. Found in Mid-Cornwall.
Bennetto	Children of Bennet or Benedict.
Benney, Binney, Bunney, Bonney, Penney	Meaning obscure, unless from bonny: cluster, clump or bunch of ores. Found generally throughout Cornwall. May have a common origin with Knee.
Berryman, Berriman	Man of St. Buryan. Name associated with Cornwall for centuries. Now found concentrated in West Cornwall not far from St. Buryan.
Bersey	Name occurs in Bodmin Manumissions as Byrsige, a priest witness. Place name Trebursey, South Petherwin.
Berty, Burthy, Bertho	From perthy: bushes. Place name Berthy in St. Enoder parish was spelt Brethei in Domesday Book and may derive from bryth, freckles or spots, from colourings of the district.
Bescoby	From bos Scoby: dwelling of Scoby (personal name). Place name Biscovey, St. Blazey.
Beskeen	From bos keyn: dwelling on the ridge. Name found in Redruth district. Alternative derivation: from bos-cun: abode of dogs.
Best	From best: moss. Name recorded in Cornwall since 17th century. Now found in China Clay district. Possible place name Lambest, Menheniot.

Beswarick	From bos gwarthek: dwelling of cattle, or Bos Worec: dwelling of Worec (personal name). Found in Mid and SE. Cornwall. Place names, Treworrick, St. Cleer; Carwarrick, Lanreath; Rosewarrick, Lanivet.
Beswetherick	From bos (g)wydhal: dwelling by the thicket, or bos Gwydhalek: dwelling of the Irishman. Found in Mid and East Cornwall.
Bevan	Of Welsh descent, ab Evan: Son of Evan.
Bew, Bewes, Buse	From bew: lively. Place name Lesbew, Sancreed.
Bice	Perhaps from bys: finger – a narrow strip of land between converging streams or tracks. Found in Newquay district. Early form: Bysse.
Biddick	Personal name Budic, from budhek: victorious. Parish name Budock. Found in NE. and Mid Cornwall. Possibly masculine form of Budhycca.
Bines	Probably a break-away from surname Carbines, and place name Carbean, St. Austell parish (spelt Carnbyhan 1327 – Carn byhan: little rock mass).
Biscombe, Buscombe	Possibly from bos-cum: valley abode.
Blamey	Probably Cornish form of Bellamy, fair friend (from French Bel ami).
Bligh, Blight, Blyth	From blyth: wolf.
Boase, Bose	Early spellings give Bores, from bos-res: the dwelling by the ford. Name first appears in Camborne Parish Register 1599. Now found concentrated in West Cornwall.
Boast, Bost	Possibly nickname from bost: brag or boast.
Boden, Boaden	From bod: dwelling, with suffix -en making a singular from collective noun, hence, dwelling in a group of dwellings. Place name Boden, St. Anthony in Meneage.
Bodenham	From bod Dynham: dwelling of Dynham. Place name Dinham, St. Minver, and parish name Cardinham.
Bodiella	From bod Ella: dwelling of Ella. Place name Bodella, St. Dennis, See Ellis, Bodilly and Dilly.

Bodilly	As Bodiella.
Bodinnar, Berdinnar	From bod Ynyr, or Ener: dwelling of Ynyr. Place name Bodinar, Sancreed. Found in West Cornwall.
Body, Boddy, Boddie	Probably from bod-dy, as a special kind of house in a dwelling place or settlement.
Bolitho	Possibly from bod plus personal name. Place names, Bolitho in Crowan and Menheniot. Found in SE. and West Cornwall. Related To Laity. Bod(D) Lethyow: dwelling with dairies?
Bone	Origin obscure. Place name Bone, Madron (spelt Boden in 1327). See Boden.
Bonney, Benney, Binney	Bonney found Mid- and East Cornwall, Benney, Binney mostly in West. Possibly as Penney, from penna: chiefest.
Bonython	From bos Nectan: dwelling of Nectan or Nighton. Place name Bonython, Cury. Also Trenython, Tywardreath.
Borlase, Burlase	From bur-(g)las: green bank. Place name Borlase, St. Wenn. Found mostly in Mid and SE. Cornwall.
Bosanketh, Bosanquet	From bos Angawd: dwelling of Angawd (personal name). Place name, Bosanketh, St. Buryan.
Bosanko	From bos ancow: dwelling of death or bos an cos: dwelling in the wood. Name originated in parishes of Crowan and Wendron.
Boscawen	From bos scawen: dwelling of the elder tree. Recorded in Helston 1327. Place name Boscawen in St. Buryan and Mawgan-in-Meneage parishes. Alternative derivation: from bos-Gawen: abode of Gawen (personal name).
Bosence	From bos syns: dwelling of the holy men, or sacred dwelling, or bos (g)wyns: dwelling of the wind. Place names Bosence in Sancreed and in St. Erth parishes.
Bosustow, Bosisto	From bos Ustoc: dwelling of Ustoc (personal name). Place name Bosustow, St. Levan. Chirgwin suggests from bos-ysow: corn abode.

Boswarva	From place name Boswarva, Madron, spelt Bos worweth in 1289, thus either the end dwelling, or dwelling of a person Gwrwydd.
Botheras	From place name Portheras, St. Just, origin Porth Eres, Cove or landing place of Eres (personal name). Found exclusively in West Cornwall.
Botterell, Bottrell, Botral	Probably originated from place name Tibida Boterel in SE. Brittany, thence to Castello Boterel in Cornwall (1284), now Boscastle. Name now found chiefly in West Cornwall.
Boundy	From bownd-dy: house by the miner's claim or tin bound. Mentioned in 1327 Register. Found in Mid and N. Cornwall.
Bowden, Bawden	Cornish form of Baudouin. Place name Bowden appears in St. Neot and Stratton parishes.
Branwell	From place name Brannel, St. Stephens, St. Austell. Bran (crow) and suffix -iel, low-lying arable land frequented by crows. (Cf. English: Crowland).
Bray	From bre: hill. Many place names Brea, Bray, Kelly Bray etc. Name widely distributed.
Britton, Britten, Briddon	Descendants of immigrants from Brittany.
Brock	From brogh: badger. Found in North, Mid and East Cornwall.
Brockenshaw, Brokenshire	Possibly from bro-kensa: first or chief region.
Buckett	From bos keth: dwelling of the serf or bondman. Original spelling Boketh.
Buddle	Corruption of the Bodell group, q.v. Found in Camborne-Redruth area.
Bullock	From bulgh and dim.-yk: thus little hare-lipped man.
Bunt	Possibly from bans: high place, cliff.
Burrows	From burow: embankments or entrenchments. Found in North and Mid Cornwall.
Buzza	From bossow: dwellings. Place name Bossow, Towednack. Found in Mid and West Cornwall.

Buzzacott	In 1399 spelling Bursecott, hence hybrid Bersey's cottage. Name Byrsige appears as that of a Celtic priest in Bodmin Manumissions.
Caddy	From ke (or cae)-dy: house surrounded by hedge. See Cardy.
Cadwalader, Cadwallader	Mentioned in 1523 Lay Subsidy Roll for Zennor parish. Name of Welsh saint, as in Welsh place name Llangadwaladr.
Cadwell	Related to Cadwallader, q.v.
Calf, Calff	From caf: cave. Name found in Ladock parish.
Cann	From can: brightness, splendour. Mention in 1327 LSR. for Crowan. Now found in North Cornwall.
Cant	See Kent. Name still extant in Cornwall.
Carah, Cara	From cara: to love or carer: lover, friend. Found in 1327 L.S.R. St. Eval.
Carbines	From carn-byhan: little rock-pile. Place name is Carbean, St. Austell, Carnbyhan in 1357.
Carbis	From car-bons: cart-bridge. Place name in Roche, St. Hilary, Stithians, and Carbis Bay. Name now found in West and South Cornwall.
Cardell	From carn-Dell: Dell's rock-pile. See Dell.
Carder	From car-dyr: land by the fort.
Cardew	From car-du: dark fort or earthwork. Place name Cardew in Trevalga and Warbstow. Name now found in West and SE. Cornwall.
Cardy, Carty, Carthy	From car-dy: house by the fort. Place name Parc-an-Caddy, St. Buryan (spelt Parke an Cardy in early documents). Related to Irish and Scottish personal name Carthy.
Care	From car: fort or camp. Place names Lancare, Pelynt; Roscare, St. Gennys; Roskear, Camborne; Gear, St. Erth etc. Found in West Cornwall.
Carew	From kerrow: forts. Place name Pencarrow, Advent.

Carey	Possibly from cara: to love, or carer: friend. See Cara. Place name River Cary tributary of the Tamar. Name now found in West Cornwall.
Cargeeg, Carkeek	From car-ke-ek: fort with hedge around it. Found in West Cornwall.
Carhart	From car-horth: fort of the ram. Place name Carhart, St. Breock, in which parish name is still found.
Carkeet	Possibly from car-keth: fort or earthwork of the serf or bondman. Place name Carkeet, St. Cleer. Compare Cargeeg, Carkeek.
Carlin	From car-lyn: fort by the pool. Place name Carleen, Mawgan in Meneage (spelt Caerlin 1250).
Carloss	From car-los: grey or hoary fort. Place name Carloose in Gwinear and Creed parishes.
Carlyon	From car-lyjyon: camp of the legion, or car-leghen: earthwork of slate or shale. Place names, Carlyon, Kea and St. Minver; Carleen, Breage; Carleon, Morval.
Carnall, Carnell	Possibly from Carn-hal: rock pile on the moor. Place name Carnhell, Gwinear. Found in Far West Cornwall.
Carne	From carn: pile of rocks. Over 100 place names prefixed by Carn. Name now evenly distributed throughout Cornwall.
Carnsew	From carn-su (variant of du): dark pile of rocks. Place name Carnsew in Mabe and St. Erth. Name found in W. Cornwall.
Carrick	From carrek: rock mass. Carrick Roads, Falmouth; Carrickowel Point, St. Austell.
Carrivick	From place name Carevick, Cubert, (spelt Crowarthevick 1529). Crow means hut or hovel but second element obscure.
Carthew	From car-du: dark camp or earthwork. Place names in St. Issey, St. Austell, Wendron and Madron parishes.

Carveth	From car- (m)vergh: camp of the horses. Place name Carveth in Cuby (spelt Carvegh in 1334). Place names Carveth in Mabe and Carvath in St. Austell gave rise to name Keveth q.v. Name found almost exclusively in Camborne-Truro area.
Carvolth	From place name Corvolth, Crowan. Carn-molgh: rock pile of the thrush.
Carwana	From place name Carwenna, Veryan. Car-whennen: camp of weeds.
Carwin, Carwyn	From car-wyn: white camp.
Case, Cass	Possibly from cas, meaning war, battle or fight. Name found in St. Austell area.
Casley, Causley	From caslys: headquarters, entrenchment. Found as Casley in West Cornwall and Causley in E. Cornwall.
Castine	Possibly from cas-tyn: cruel war. Possible place name Castinnicks, Isles of Scilly.
Cattran	Cornish form of Catherine.
Cavell, Cavill	Possibly Cyvel, personal name, or from Kevellek: woodcock. Place name Nanskeval. See also Nankivell. Possibly from obsolete Cornish keval: horse (cf. W. ceffyl).
Cawrse	From cors: fen, reed grown bog. Place name Pencorse, St. Enoder. Found in SE. Cornwall.
Challis, Callis, Collis	Possibly from goles: bottom or lowest part. See Nancollas.
Charke	Origin obscure. There is a dialect word cherk: ashes. Place name Charke, Lanlivery. Name found in Liskeard-Looe area.
Chegwidden, Chegwin, Chegwyn	From chy gwyn: white house. Place name Chegwidden, Constantine. Found in Mid and West Cornwall.
Chellew	From chy logh: house by the lake or inlet of water, or chy Lew: house of Lew. Found in Far-West Cornwall.
Chenery	Pronounced Chy-nerr-y. From Chy'nerewey: house in acres (or within boundaries). See Trenerry.

Chenhall	From chy'n hal: house on the moor. Place name Chynhale, Wendron and Perranzabuloe parishes.
Chenhalls	From chy'n als: house on the cliff or shore. Place name Chenalls, St. Erth.
Chenoweth, Chynoweth	From chy noweth: new house. Place name in many parishes. Found mainly in Mid. West Cornwall.
Chirgwin	From (chy) gour gwyn, (house of) the fair man. Found mainly in Far West Cornwall.
Chivell	Possibly from chy aval: house of apple or from chy vylas: cattle house. Place name Chyvelah, Kenwyn.
Chivers, Cheffers, Chiffers	From chy fer: house by the fair (market).
Chiverton	From chy war ton: house on the unploughed grassland. Name common 16th century. Place names Chiverton, Perranzabuloe and Illogan; Chivarton, St. Buryan.
Choak	From chok: jackdaw (or chatterer). Found West of Truro.
Clegg	Possibly from clegh: bells, hence, bell-ringer.
Clemmow, Clemo, Climo, Clymo	Of Clement's family.
Clews	This name appears to be a breakaway from Carclew, Mylor (Crucleu in 1311), from Cruc: barrow and Lew: personal name, as W. Llew-ellyn.
Clinnick	Possibly from lonek: bushy place (cf. W. Clynog: brakes and bushes). Place name Clennick, Bradoc and St. Germans.
Clogg	From clog: crag or cliff. Found in East Cornwall.
Cloke, Clook	From clog: crag or cliff, or from clogh: bell. Found in Mid and East Cornwall.
Clymas	Possibly originated from place name Clims, Stoke Climsland. Meaning perhaps from clegar: cliff, slope.
Coad, Coode	From cos: wood, or from coth: old. See Coath.

Coath	Appears to be original form of Coad and Coode. From coth: old, hence perhaps, eldest son. Found in Liskeard-Looe area.
Cock	Possibly from cok: sailing boat or from cok: empty, vain.
Cogar	Possibly from chogha: jackdaw, hence chatterer. Found as Cogar in 1324, now found in S.W Cornwall. Place name Kuggar, Grade (also spelt Coger in 1324).
Colenso	From ke lyn du: the dark, hedged pool. Place name Colenso, St. Hilary.
Collett	From collwyth: hazel trees. Place name Nancolleth, Newlyn East. Found in Mid and West Cornwall. Name appears to have originated in Roseland. 86 marriages of Collett there 1600-1812.
Colley, Collie, Colly, Colle	From coll-egy: hazel place.
Collick, Collict	From coll-yk: little hazel. Found in St. Stephen in Brannel.
Collis	From coll-ys: lower hazel grove.
Colliver	From coll-egy-va: place of hazels. Found in Mid Cornwall.
Colquite	From kyl-cos(quite): back of wood. Place name Colquite in Callington and Lanteglos-by-Fowey.
Combellack	Originally Carnebellack. Possibly from carn pellek: rounded rock pile. Found in Mid West Cornwall.
Congdon	Perhaps from corn dyn: corner fort? Place name Congdon, South Petherwin. Found in East Cornwall.
Conner	Personal name Conor. Place names Treconner, South Hill and Connerton, Gwithian.
Connock, Cunnack, Cunnick	From connek: clever, skilful or from personal name Conoc. Place name Boconnoc.
Coombe, Coombes	From cum: little valley. Many place names with this element. Name now found evenly distributed throughout Cornwall.

Coon	From cun: dogs, hounds or from Cun: chief, lord. Only important people kept hounds, so, perhaps the two meanings are related. Name found in Mid Cornwall.
Copp	Possibly from cop: summit. Compare place names Boscoppa, St. Austell (Boscobb in 1362, dwelling on summit) and Polscopp, St. Neot. Found in Gerrans and SE. Cornwall.
Corey, Cory	Possibly from cor-e(g)y: corner place. Place name Curry, Boyton.
Corin	Possibly from cor-yn: in a corner. See Corey and Curry. Found in West Cornwall.
Cornish, Cornwall	From A.S. Corn-wealas: stranger of the horn, headland; name given by Saxons to people of Kernow.
Cossentine	From parish and personal name Constantine.
Cothey	From coth-e(g)y, old place. Alternative derivation: from cothhe: to grow old.
Cottell, Cotell, Cottle	From place name Cotehele, Calstock cos-hayl: wood by the estuary. Found in North Cornwall.
Couch	From cough: red (? nickname for auburn-haired). Widely distributed throughout Cornwall.
Cowling	Possibly from cawlen: cabbage, or diminuitive of Colyn or Nicholas.
Cowls, Coules, Coulls	From cowel: basket or pannier. Found in West Cornwall.
Craddock, Cradick	Personal name Caradoc. Place name Rosecraddock, St. Cleer. Found in Mid and East Cornwall.
Crago	From crugyow: barrows, mounds. Place names Cregoe, Ruan Lanihorne and Crugoes, Colan. Found in Mid and East Cornwall.
Craggs, Craig	From carrek: rock mass. Found in Mid Cornwall.
Crapp	Still extant in East Cornwall. Possibly from crapya: to grip, or a varient of Greep, q.v.
Craze	From cres: middle (of a place). Found in Mid and West Cornwall.

Crebo, Creba	From crybow: crests, ridges. Place name Polcrebo, Crowan. Found in West Cornwall.
Creed	From parish names Creed and Sancreed.
Creek	From cruk: mound, barrow. Place name Tencreek, Menheniot and Trencreek, St. Columb Minor. Found in West Cornwall.
Crocker, Croker	Derivation uncertain, possibly from old plural of carrek: rocks. Place name Pennycrocker, St. Juliot.
Croggan	Probably from croghen: skin, hide, leather. Or from Crogen: skull. Place name Roscroggan, Camborne. Found at Grampound as name of well-known tanners.
Crowgey	From crow-chy: hut-house, or one roomed cottage. Place name in Gwennap, Wendron, Constantine and Ruan Minor. Found in West Cornwall.
Crowle	Possibly from crow(le): cottager. Found in Mid Cornwall.
Cuff, Cuffe	From cuf: dear, kind.
Cullum	From parish name, St. Columb. Found in Mid Cornwall.
Cundy	From cun dy: house where dogs were bred. Found in Mid and SE. Cornwall.
Curgenven	From car-Cenwyn: camp of Kenwyn (personal name). Place name Cargenwen, Crowan. Parish name Kenwyn.
Curnow	From Kernow, Cornishman. May be name given to descendants of Irish Kerns, invaders of 5th century. Found in Far West Cornwall.
Currow	Still found in Mid-Cornwall. From currow: borders of country.
Curry, Currie	Said to be old stream name, but meaning uncertain. See Cory. Found in West Cornwall.
Curtis, Courtis, Courtice, Corteys, Courties	From either cortys, meaning courts; or cortes, meaning courteous. Evenly distributed throughout Cornwall.

Daddow	Either diminutive from David, or derived from da: good, thus good fellow.
Dannan, Danning	From place name Bodannan, St. Endellion, meaning dwelling of Annan (personal name). See Annan, Anning.
Dean, Deane	From den: man. See Andain, Endean. Found widely distributed throughout Cornwall.
Dell	Probably personal name Dell, as in Bodell, Cardell. Found in Camborne and Bude areas.
Denham, Dynham, Dinham	Possibly from dynyon: hill-forts. Place name Cardinham. Name well known in 16th – 18th cents. in Bodmin-Bude area.
Derrick	From derowek: oak grove. Not related to Dowrick.
Derry	From derow: oak trees. Place name Eglosderry, Wendron. Found in Mid Cornwall.
Deveril, Deveral	From Dever (variant of dowr)-iel: water, or stream within fertile banks Place names Deveral, Gwinear; Deverel, Sancreed.
Dew	From du: black, dark, sombre. Found in Launceston.
Dilly	Personal name. Place name Bodilly, Wendron, dwelling of Dili.
Dinner, Denner	Breton Saint's name Diner. Place name Landinner, Altarnun. Found in NE. Cornwall.
Dobell, Doble	Meaning obscure, bell: distant, as in Abell. Found in Mid and Mid-West Cornwall.
Dolley	Probably from dol-y(n); narrow meadow with stream. Found exclusively in SE. Cornwall.
Dow	First found in 18th cent. Scottish Gaelic form of Cornish du: dark, black.
Dowell	From Scots Gaelic dowel: dark stranger.
Dower	From dowr: water. Place names Dower, Crowan; Dowran, St. Just in Penwith; Poldower, Tregoney. Found in Mid and West Cornwall.
Dowling, Dowlyn	From deulyn: knees. Possibly nickname.

Dowrick	From dowrack: watery place, or dowr-yk: little water. Found in Mid Cornwall.
Drake	Found generally in Cornwall from 16th century onwards. Origin unknown. Place name Landrake was spelt Landerhtune in 1018, possibly from lanherch: glade, clear space. Found in many places in Cornwall.
Dray	From tre: homestead. Place names e.g. Pendrea, St. Buryan; Tredrea, St. Erth. See also Pondray, Tredrea.
Drew	Obscure, unless from tro: turn, twist. Place name Cardrew, Redruth, spelt Caerdro in 1311. Found in West Cornwall. Gover suggests from W. dryw: wren. May be late form of Germanic personal name Drogo, via French form Dreus. Druce Thomas mentioned in 1523 LSR.
Dungey	Derivation obscure unless from dyn-jy: house by hill-fort. Found in Mid and West Cornwall.
Dustow	Parish name Davidstow (pronounced locally Dewstow) or personal name Ustoc, as in place name Bosustow, St. Levan, from Bod-Ustoc, dwelling of Ustoc. Found only in Camborne-Redruth.
Dyer	From tyor: thatcher.
Ead, Eade, Ede	Found from 16th century onwards, now in Mid and SE. Cornwall. Possibly from personal name Ide. There is parish in Devon named Ide (pronounced Eed).
Eathorne	From eythyn: furze-bush. Place name Eathorne, Mabe. Found in Mid-West Cornwall.
Eddy	Possibly from Ede-dy: Ede's house. Mid and West Cornwall.
Edyvean, Eddyvean	Possibly from Edno-vyhan: little Uthno, as in Ednovean, Perranuthnoe. Or from Ide-dy-vyhan: little house of Ide. Found in Mid and North Cornwall. Alternative derivation, from Udy-vyghan: son of Udy or Eda.
Ellacott, Ellicoat, Elcoat	Elli is personal name, hence hybrid Cornish-A.S. Elli's cottage. Found in East Cornwall, where A.S first supplanted Cornish.

Ellens	From elyn: corner, elbow or from elyl: as in place name Ellenglaze, Cubert, spelt Elil, Domesday Book, probably plot of ground.
Ellery	From elergh(y): swans. Parish name Veryan was Elerchi in Domesday Book, later elerghy. Found in Mid and North Cornwall.
Elliott	Again from personal name Elli.
Ellis	From personal name Elli - hence, children of Elli.
Ennis, Enys	From enys: island, isolated place, peninsula. Place names Ennis, St. Enoder and Tregoney; Enys, St. Gluvias; Ennys, St. Hilary. See also Innis.
Ennor	From an – or: the boundary, or from enor: honour.
Eustace, Eustice	From Parish name St. Just. Found in West Cornwall.
Eva, Evea	Celtic personal name Hyviu. Place names Trevio, St. Merryn; Goneva, Gwinear (spelt Gwynhybyowe 1400). Found mostly in Mid West Cornwall.
Evans	Celtic form of John. Found in Registers from 16th century onwards. Evenly distributed throughout Cornwall.
Faull	Possibly from fall: fail, fault, deficiency. Recorded marriages early 16th century, Crowan parish. Still found mostly within 10 miles of that parish. Alternative derivation, from faw-la: place of beeches.
Fenton	From fenten: spring or well. Place names numerous, e.g. Ventongimps, Zelah. See also Venton.
Fiddick,Fidock	From personal name Budhyk, or from budhek: victorious.
Floyd, Flood	From personal name Lloyd. Found in West Cornwall.
Foss	From fos: wall, rampart, ditch. Place name Marazanvose, St. Allen (Marghas an Vos, market on the rampart). Found in West Cornwall.
Found	Probably breakaway from Penfound, Otterham (Penfoun 1356) and derived from fawen: beech tree. Still found in North Cornwall.

Frayne	Possibly from bran: crow. Found in N.E. Cornwall.
Freethy	From freth: eager, eloquent, alert. Name recorded in 1327 L.S.R. Crantock. Alternative derivation, from place name Freethy in Antony. 18 Freethy marriages recorded in that area in 16th cent.
Friggens	Possibly nickname from fregys: tatterdemalion (ragged person). Found in Far West Cornwall.
Fry	Derivation Obscure. Place name Treffry in Merther, St. Gluvias and Lanhydrock parishes. Found in North Cornwall. Possibly from vry: worth.
Gale, Gall, Galley	Possibly from Gall, denoting Frenchman. Place name Trengale, St. Cleer (Trengalla 1201, homestead of the Frenchman). Found in East Cornwall mainly.
Garland	Breakaway from place name Tregarland, Morval (in 1198 spelt Crug-alyn: mound or barrow of Alyn).
Gay	From ke: hedge or fence. Place name Tregea, Illogan. Found in Mid and Mid West Cornwall.
Geach	Origin obscure. Possibly a personal name. Well established since 16th century. Now found in Mid and SE. Cornwall.
Geake	Possibly from ke-ek: hedged, hence builder of hedges. Found in E. Cornwall.
Gear	From an ger: the hill-fort, earthwork. Place name Gear in many parishes, e.g. Camborne, St. Erth, St. Ewe.
Gee	Derivation uncertain. Place name Bogee, St. Ervan, was spelt Bosyuf 1340, and second element probably personal name.
Gerrans	From parish name Gerrans, named after Cornish King-Saint Gerent or Geraint.
Gew	From kew: enclosure. Place name Gew in Crowan, St. Erth and Kea.
Giddy, Gedye	From gedyer: guide, leader. Found East Cornwall.
Gillis	Possibly derived from gell: brown, tawny. Place names Tregillis, S. Petherwin; Pensagillis, St. Ewe. Compare Tregellas.

Glass	From glas: blue, green, grey, pale.
Glasson	From glesyn: grass plot. Found in West Cornwall.
Glinn, Glynn	From glyn: deep valley. Place name Glynn, Cardinham.
Gloyn, Gloyne	From glow-en: charcoal. Found in East Cornwall.
Glubb	Jenner suggests nickname from glyb: damp, moist.
Gluyas	Parish name, St. Gluvias. Still found mostly within a few miles of that parish.
Goard	Found in Cornwall over many centuries.
Godden, Gooden	It has been suggested that this is a diminutive of cod (Breton kod), meaning bag, in the sense of a hollow. Place name Tregooden, St. Tudy.
Godolphin	From godolghyn: rising ground, or tump. Place name Godolphin, Breage.
Goff, Gough	Found in North and East Cornwall. Possibly from cough: red. Goff appears in 1523 LSR.
Goldsworthy	Possibly from gol-erewy: field of feast or fair. Name appears as Golsery 1680. Place name Goldsworthy in Crowan and Gwennap. Found West of Truro.
Golley, Gollie	From gol-ey: feast or fair place. Found in Mid Cornwall.
Goninan	From ke-onnen: hedge of ash trees. Accent is on 'in'. Place name Tregonnan, Mawgan in Pydar.
Gool, Gole	From goles: bottom. Place name Tregole, Otterham. Found in Mid Cornwall.
Gordon	Appears as second element of place name Tregordon, Egloshayle, and may be derived from a personal name or from gordhyans: honour.
Goss	From cors: fen, reed-bog. Place name Tregoss, Roche. Found in Mid and SE. Cornwall.
Gover, Govier	From gover: brook, stream. Place names Gover, St. Agnes; Pengover, Menheniot; Pengovier, Morval.
Govett	Possibly from goves: smiths.
Greep, Gripe	From an gryb: crest or ridge. Place name Pengreep, Gwennap.

Greet	From an (c) grug (t): mound, barrow. Place name Parc an Greet, St. Ives.
Grey, Gray	From gre: flock, herd, hence herdsman. Place names Tregray, Otterham; Polgray, Altarnun.
Gribbin, Gribben, Gripe	From cryb-yn: narrow ridge or crest. Name appears to have originated St. Agnes, and is chiefly found in the area today. Place name Gribbin Head.
Gribble	From cryb-a-bell: the distant ridge, early spelling being Gribbell. Found Mid and West Cornwall.
Griffin, Griffiths	Though of Welsh origin this name has been recorded in Cornwall for at least 4 centuries. Found chiefly in Mid and West Cornwall.
Grigg, Gregg	From gregga: to cackle, hence nickname. Found in Mid Cornwall.
Grose	From an grows: the cross. Place name e.g. Trengrouse, Veryan; Angrouse, Mullion. Found in Mid Cornwall.
Grylls, Grills	Derivation obscure. Perhaps from gryll: a cricket. Place names Tregrylls, Lesnewth; Tregirls, Altarnun. Found in NE and SE. Cornwall.
Gue	From an gew: the enclosure, field. Place name Gew found in Crowan, Kea, St. Erth.
Gummow, Gummoe	From cummow: little valleys. Place name Gummow, Probus. Found in M Cornwall.
Gundry	From gun-dre: homestead on the down. Found Mid West and SE. Cornwall.
Gwavas	From gwavas: winter abode, permanent farmstead.
Gwennap	From Parish name Gwennap, dedication St. Weneppa. Found in Far West Cornwall.
Gwinnel	Possibly from gwennol: swallow. Place name Tregwindles, St. Breock (spelt Tregwynnel 1280). Found in St. Austell.
Gwynn	From gwyn: white, fair, bright. Found in small scattered groups in 7 parishes. See Angwin.

Hain, Hayne, Haines, Heynes	Possibly from hen: old. Place name Trehane in David-stow and Probus, were spelt Treyahan in 1288, and second element may be form of John.
Hair, Hare	From hyr: long, hence tall man. Found mostly in East Cornwall.
Hale	From hal: moor. Place name Penhale in more than 20 parishes.
Hammett	Possibly from early form of hewas: summer dwelling. Place names Hammett, Quethiock; Hampt, Stoke Climsland. Found Mid & North Cornwall.
Hammill	Personal name Hamil. Compare Hamilton, Scottish place name. Found in Mid West Cornwall. Possibly of Hugenot origin, but found in Cornwall from 1711 onwards. Place name Trehamel, Gerrans.
Hampton	Derivation uncertain – possibly from Hampt, Stoke Climsland or similar place further West. Now found mostly west of Truro.
Hancock	From hen – gok: great grandfather, ancestor.
Hannaford	Appears to be a hybrid Cornish x English name. Found mostly in East Cornwall, where Hannafore, Looe is a place name.
Hannah, Hennah	From henna: older or personal name as in Behenna Found in Mid Cornwall.
Hart	Derivation obscure, but possibly from horth: ram, thus a nickname. Found in West Cornwall.
Harvey	Possibly from Breton haer-vy: battle worthy, or Cornish arva: to arm. Original Harveys would appear to have been warriors. Widely distributed throughout Cornwall, mainly concentrated in West.
Heale, Heal	From hel: hall, hence worker in manor hall. Place name Penheale, Egloskerry. Found in West & East Cornwall.
Hearn, Hearne, Horne	From horn (plural, hern): iron: hence possibly iron-miner. Found in Mid-West & S. E. Cornwall.

Hellen (S), Hellings, Hellyns	Found 16th and 17th cents. Newlyn East, St Gluvias? From adjective hel: generous, hospitable?
Hellyer	Possibly from Dialect hellyer: slater or from helghyer: huntsman.
Hender, Hendra	From hendra: fixed habitation, or hen-dre: old homestead. Found in East Cornwall.
Henderson	Possibly from hendra: old place, hence son of Hendra, q.v.
Hendy	From hen-dy: old house. Found in West Cornwall.
Hendry	Still extant in East Cornwall and Plymouth areas. From hen-dra: old place.
Hobba, Hobby	From hobba: riding horse, hence horseman. Place name Stable Hobba, Newlyn West.
Hocken, Hocking	Originated in Cornwall, if not Celtic, appearing frequently in records from 1523, as Huchyn, apparently a pet name. Found in great numbers in West and Mid Cornwall.
Hollow	From hallow: moors. Place name Hallow, Roche: many Penhallows. Found in West Cornwall.
Honey	Contraction of Hannibal.
Horne	From horn: iron. Compare Kinghorn: man of iron. See Hearn.
Hosken, Hosking, Hoskins	From heskyn: sedge-marsh. Found mostly in Mid and West Cornwall, though in numbers in many areas.
Howell	Personal name Howel. Howel was the last native King of Cornwall. Found in Mid Cornwall.
Huddy	From huth-dy: shady house. Found Mid and East Cornwall.
Hugh, Hughes	From personal name Hugh, or perhaps from ugh (prefix): high.
Hunkin	Derivation unknown, but evidently a diminutive. Found in Mevagissey area.
Hurdon	Place name Hurdon, Altarnun. Origin obscure.

Hutchens, Hichens, Houchen	Diminutive of Hugh. Well distributed.
Huthnance	From huth-nans: shady, sheltered valley. Found in West Cornwall.
Ince	From enys: island, isolated place. Cf. Enys, Annis.
Inch, Innes, Innis	From enys: island or isolated place. Place name Innis, Lanlivery.
Isbell	From ys-bell: lower, distant (some distance down the hill). Found in Mid and SE. Cornwall.
Ive, Ivey, Ivy	Parish name St. Ive, or place name Ivey, St. Breward (spelt Hethia 1282, hence perhaps from ydhyow: Ivy). Found West Cornwall.
Jago, Jaco, Jacka	Cornish form of James. Place name Treago, Crantock; Trago, St. Pinnock, both spelt Treiagu in 13th century. Found West and SE. Cornwall.
Jelbart, Jelbert	Cornish form of Gilbert.
Jenner	Chirgwin suggests from jynor: engineer, but this doubtful.
Jewell, Jewells	Celtic personal name as Judhall, a royal name. Cornish jowal: jewel. Evenly distributed throughout.
Joll, Jolliffe, Juleff, Jolly	From jolyf: lively, gay, pleasant. Found in Mid and SE. Cornwall.
Jory	Cornish form of George.
Jose	Romano-Celtic surname, borrowed from Latin Joseus during Roman occupation. Well known in 14th century.
Julian, Julyan	Another Romano-Celtic surname, well established in 1327.
Keast, Keats	From kest: straw basket, hence, perhaps basket maker. Found in Mid and North Cornwall.
Keat, Keith	From keth: slave, serf or bondman. Found in SE. Cornwall, and Padstow area.
Keel	From kel: shelter, bower. Place name Carkeel, St. Stephens, by Saltash.

Keen, Keane	From ky-yn: little dog or plural cun: dogs. Place names Carkean, St. Teath; Roskean, St. Merryn.
Keigwin	From ky-gwyn: white dog. Doble suggests possibly from ke-gwyn: blessed St. Kea.
Kelly, Kellow	From kelly, kellyow (plural): grove or groves. Place names numerous, e.g. Treskellow, Treneglos; Kellow, Lansallos; Kelly Bray, Stoke Climsland. Found in Mid-West, Mid and North Cornwall.
Kelynack	From kelynek: holly grove. See also Clinnick. Found in Far West Cornwall.
Kemp	Possibly from kempen: neat, tidy. Well established in Middle Ages. Found in Mid West Cornwall.
Kempthorne	Possibly from kempen: neat, tidy. Thron may mean nose or point of land. Could be nickname.
Kent	Originated in St. Minver parish, where name was taken from Latin Canti: corner, hence people of the corner (as in Kent). Place name Cant, St. Minver. Found in Mid and North Cornwall.
Kernick	From kernyk: little corner. Place name Kernick in 9 parishes. Found in Far West Cornwall.
Kersey	From kersy: fens, reed-grown bogs. Place name Nankersey, Mylor.
Keskeys	From ker-skewys: sheltered camp. See Skewes. Found in Far West Cornwall.
Kestle, Kestell, Kessell	From kestel (castel): earthwork or castle. Place name Kestle in 7 parishes. Found in Mid and North Cornwall.
Keverne	Parish name St. Keverne. Found in Mid West Cornwall.
Keveth	From ker-(m)vergh: camp of horses. See Carveth. Found in St. Austell area.
Key	From Parish name Kea.
Killick	From culyek: cock. Place name Trekillick, Lanivet.
Killigrew	Probably from kelly-gre: grove of flock or herd.

Kimber	From kembrek, Welsh. Established for 6 centuries.
Kingdon	Possibly from cun-dyn: chief fort. Place name Kingdon, Antony. Found in Mid, SE. and North Cornwall.
Kinghorn	From kyn-hoern: iron chief. See Polkinghorne.
Kinsey	Possibly from kensa: first, foremost. Place names River Kensey, Launceston; Bokenso, Gwithian.
Kinver	From cun-va: dogs' place (where dogs were bred). Found in Mid SE. and North Cornwall.
Kirby	Possibly from cryb – ek: ridged, crested. Place name Treskerby, Gwennap (spelt Treskrebig 1394).
Kitto, Kittow	Kit is pet name for Christopher, hence Kitto, Kit's children.
Kivell	Possibly personal name Gyfel or perhaps from place name Nanskeval, Mawgan in Pydar (spelt Nanscuvel 1277) or from parish name St. Michael Penkevil.
Kliskey	From cowl-lesky: burn up completely.
Kneebone	Breakaway from Carnebone, Wendron (spelt Carnebwen 1298 – hence Ebwen's rock-pile). Chirgwin suggests alternative derivation from carn-ebol: colt corral.
Knuckey	From kenegen: boggy place, spring head. Place name Kenegie, Gulval; Keneggy, Germoe.
Laity	From leth-ty: milk house (dairy). Place name in 7 parishes. Found in West Cornwall.
Lambourne	From lan bron: enclosure of hill. Place name Lambriggan, Perranzabubloe (spelt Lanbronwegha 1339).
Lambrick	As Lambourne, from Lan-bron-wyk: enclosure of hill village or wood. Found South Cornwall.
Lampier	From lan-plu: parish enclosure. Place name Namplough, Cury (Lamploigh 1334).
Lander, Launder Ladner	From lan-der(tyr): churchyard or glebe. Chirgwin suggests from lan-dar: oak enclosure. Found in Far West, East and North Cornwall.

Landeryou, Lenderyou	From lyn-derow: pool by oak trees. Place name Landerio, Mylor. Found in Falmouth area.
Landry, Landrey, Laundry	From lan-dre: homestead by enclosure or glebe. Found in East Cornwall.
Lanfear	Possibly from lan-fer: feast or fair enclosure, or from Welsh Llanfair.
Lansallos	From parish name Lansallos- Lan Salwys, enclosure of St. Salwys. See also Sallos.
Lanyon	From lyn-yeyn: cold pool or lake. Place name Lanyon in Madron, Gwinear and Illogan. Found in West Cornwall.
Lavin	Possibly from leven: smooth, even. Found in Mid Cornwall.
Lawry, Lawrey, Lewry, Lowry, Lory	Possibly Derived from old Welsh Llywri: ruler, King. Or form of Lawrence. Place name, Trelawry, Manaccan. Found West and Mid Cornwall.
Leah	From lyha: least, smallest.
Lean	From lyn: stitch of land. Place names Lean in Liskeard, and St. Martin in Meneage; Penlean, Otterham; Polean, Pelynt. Frequent field name. Found Mid Cornwall.
Leaver, Lever	Possibly personal name, Lliver in Welsh. Place names Treleaver, St. Keverne (Treliver 1327); Treliever, Mabe. Found in North Cornwall.
Leddra	From leder: steep slope, cliff. Place name Leddra, St. Austell and Grade; Nancledra, Ludgvan. Found in St. Ives area.
Lee	Possibly from legh: flat stone. See Leigh, Legg.
Legassick	From lagasek: big-eyed. Place name Legassick, St. Issey is probably derived from logosek, mouse-infested.
Legg	From legh: flat rock, ledge. Found mostly in Far West Cornwall and Isles of Scilly.
Leggo	From leghow: flat rocks, ledges. Place names Treliggo, Breage, Ponsleggo, Perranzabuloe. Found in West Cornwall.

Leigh	Also from legh: flat rock, ledge. Place names Boleigh, St. Buryan, Treleigh, Lanivet, Treleigh parish, Redruth.
Lelean, Lethlean	From leth (milk)-lyn (slip or stitch of land): hence perhaps narrow dairy farm. Place name Lethlean, Phillack.
Lemin, Lemon	From place name Lemin, Gwinear (Nansmyn 1320). Nans: valley, myn: edge, hence, edge of a valley. Found in Mid and SE. Cornwall.
Lethaby, Lethby	140 marriages in 17th and 18th Cents. Mostly in East Cornwall. Possibly from leth-va: milk place, dairy. Cf. Laity.
Lethbridge	Meaning obscure, unless hybrid legh-bridge: bridge of flat rocks. Found in Isles of Scilly and in small groups elsewhere.
Lewarne, Lewin	From place name Lewarne, St. Neot, (spelt Lanwern D.B. 1086) lan-gwern: enclosure of alders; or from lewern: foxes. Found mostly SE. and North Cornwall.
Lewis	Personal name.
Ley, Lay	From legh: flat rock, ledge. Place name Ley, Linkinhorne. Found SE. and North Cornwall.
Liddicoat	Cot: wood. Lidi: possibly personal name.
Lidgey	From lughy: calves. Place name Lidgey, St. Gluvias. Found Mid Cornwall.
Light	Possibly from legh-tes: warm flat stone or ledge. Place name Trelights, St. Endellion.
Lloyd	From Welsh llwyd: grey. Found in Cornwall prior to 17th century. Cornish equivalent Loze, q.v.
Lock, Locke	Possibly from lok: monastic cell. Place name Trelocke, Menheniot. Found Mid and SE. Cornwall.
Logan	Possibly from parish name Illogan. Other place name Boderlogan, Wendron.
Lower, Lawer	From lowarth: garden, or personal name Llywarch. Place name Treloar, Wendron (Trelowargh 1336). Found Mid Cornwall.

Loy	Personal Name, Recorded in Bodmin Gospels. Place name Treloy, St. Columb Minor.
Loze	From los: grey. Place name Carloose, Creed and Gwinear parishes.
Lugg	From lugh: calf. Place name Trelugga, Ruan Major (spelt Treluga 1317 hence calf breeding farm).
Lukey, Lukeys	Personal name Lywci appears in Bodmin Gospels.
Lutey	From lugh ty: calf house. See also Lugg, Lidgey. Found in Far West Cornwall.
Luzmoor, Luzmore	Possibly from los: grey and Mor, personal name recorded in Bodmin Gospels.
Lyne, Line	From lyn: slip or stitch of land. Place names Penlyne, Lanreath; Carleen, Mawgan in Meneage (spelt Caerlin 1250). Widely distributed throughout Cornwall.
Lyon	Probably breakaway from place name Carlyon, St Minver. Still mostly found in North Cornwall.
Mabin, Mabane, Mavin	From parish name St. Mabyn. Other place name Nance-mabyn, Probus.
Mablin	From map-lyen: clerk, clergyman.
Maddern, Madron	From parish name Madron. Mostly found within 10 miles of that parish today.
Maddock	From personal name Madoc. Place names Tremadoc, St. Neot; Marsland, Morwenstowe (Maddokeslonde 1288); Culmadoc, Lanhydrock. Found Mid and E. Cornwall.
Magor, Meagor	From magor: ruin, old walls. Widely distributed.
Maile, Male	Possibly from personal name Mael, derived from meglos: prince. Place names Tremail, Davidstowe and Lanivet; Lemail, Egloshayle. Found SE. and North Cornwall.
Maker	From magor: ruin, old walls, or from parish name Maker. Found East Cornwall.

Manhire, Minear,	From men-hyr: long stone. Place names Menhire, Gwennap; Tremenheere, Stithians and Mennear, St. Austell. Found in St. Austell area.
Mankee	Possibly from men-ky: stone dog.
Mannel, Manuel	Cornish form of Emmanuel or from place name Manuells, St. Columb Minor (Maenhuwols 1289, possibly men-hewol, stone of vigilance, or watchman's lookout).
Marrack	From marghak: knight, rider.
Marshall	Chirgwin suggests from margh + ?: horse doctor, vet, but this is very doubtful.
Mayne, Maine, Main	From men: stone. Parish name Tremaine. Widely distributed.
Menadue	From meneth du: dark hill. Place names Menadue, Tintagel; Menadew, St. Breward; St. Cleer, Lanlivery; Menadews, St. Clement; Menerdue, Stithians. Found mostly North Cornwall.
Menague	From place name Meneage, Helston district. Origin managh (plural menegh): monk.
Menhenick, Menhinick, Menhenitt	Parish name Menheniot, from meneghy -Niet : sanctuary of St. Neot. Found Mid, SE. and North Cornwall.
Merrick	From morek: maritime. Place name Crigmurrick, St. Merryn (Cruckmorek 1286).
Merrin	From parish name St. Merryn. Place name Nancemerryn, Mawgan in Meneage.
Messa, Messer	Possibly from messa: to gather acorns.
Mildren	Early 18th cent. West Cornwall. From Breton?
Mitchelmore	From Myghal-mur: great St. Michael. Found North Cornwall.
Moon	From mon: slender, slim.
Moor, Moore	Possibly from mur: great, big, unless English. Widely distributed throughout Cornwall.

Morcom, Morcomb, Morcum	From mor-cum: sea coombe, valley leading to the sea. Found in Mid Cornwall.
Morgan	From Welsh personal name, but recorded as surname in Cornwall prior to 1600. Widely distributed.
Morris, Morrish	Personal name. Appears in documents 1327 onwards. Widely distributed.
Mounter	From mun-tyr: mineral land. Place name Polla-mounter, Newlyn East. See Pellymounter.
Moyle	From mol: bald, bare. Found mostly Mid Cornwall.
Mundy	From mun-dy: mineral house, hence mine house. Place name Rosemundy, St. Agnes. Found in West Cornwall.
Murray	Probably from Scottish county Moray.
Mylor	From parish name Mylor (St. Melor).
Nancarrow	From nans-carow: valley of deer or stag. Place name Nancarrow, St. Allen and St. Michael Penkevil. Found Mid and Mid West Cornwall.
Nance	From nans: valley. Place name Nance in Lelant, St. Clement, Illogan, St. Martin in Meneage.
Nancollas, Nanchollas	From nans-goles: bottom of the valley. Place name Nancolleth, Newlyn East. Found Mid West Cornwall.
Nankervis	From nans-kervys: valley of stags or deer. Place name Nankervis, St. Enoder. Found in Far West Cornwall.
Nankivell, Nancekivell	From nans-Cyfel: valley of Cyfel personal name, or possibly nans-ceffyl (Welsh), valley of horse. Place name Nanskeval, Mawgan in Pydar (Nanscuvel 1277). Found Mid West and N. Cornwall.
Nanscawen	From nans-scawen: valley of elder trees. Place name Nanscawn, Luxulyan. Found in SE. Cornwall.
Negus	From know-gos: nut-grove. Name appears as Negatus in 1327 LSR Kenwyn, so possibly from neghys: denied.
Newth	From noweth: new (newcomer?). Place names Lesnewth; Trenuth, Davidstowe; Trenewth, Lesnewth.

Ninnis	From an enys: the island or isolated place. Place names Innis and Ninnis in 15 parishes. Found in Far West Cornwall.
Noall, Nowell, Noel	Name in use in Cornwall for at least 6 centuries. Probably ancestors born at Christmas.
Noon	From an un: the down, or unenclosed land.
Noy	From noy: nephew, or from personal names Loy or Noah (Noye). Place name Nancenoy, Constantine. Found in Far West Cornwall.
Oates, Oatey	Found in Cornwall up to early 17th cent. as Otes or Otey. Possibly from German Audo (later Otho) meaning rich.
Odgers	From personal name Roger. Possibly from Germanic personal name Odger: wealth spear, but may have come into Cornish through Breton.
Old, Olds, Olde, Owles	From als: cliff, shore, strand.
Olver, Olverman, Over	From golva: watch place, lookout. Place names Penolva, St. Ives; Penolver, Landewednack; Carnolva, Sennen; Penolva, Paul. Found in Mid and SE. Cornwall.
Onion	Personal name Enyan.
Opie	Oby, diminutive for Osbert. Name originated in Cornwall. Found in Mid and West Cornwall.
Paddy	Pet form of Patrick, in use in Cornwall since 1327.
Palamountain	Varient of Pellymounter, q.v. now found in USA and Australia.
Pascoe	From Pask: Easter, hence Easter children. Name found in more than 100 places in Cornwall.
Pawley, Pawle, Paulle	Cornish form of Paul.
Pearn, Pearne	Probably a breakaway from place name Trespearne in Laneast and Sheviock parishes – tre-spernen: homestead of thorns. Still found in SE. Cornwall.

Pellow, Pellew	Possibly from pell: distant far off or from pelyow: balls, possibly nickname for round figure or head. Found in West Cornwall.
Pellymounter, Polmounter	From pol-mun-tyr: pool by the mineral land. Place Name Pollamounter, Newlyn East.
Pelmear, Polmear	Possibly from pol-mur: big pool, or as place-name Polmear, St. Austell (Porthmuer 1403 – big beach or cove).
Penaluna	From pen-lynnow: end or head of pools. Found in West Cornwall. Alternative derivation: from pen-lonnow: end of grove or bushes. Place name Luna, St. Neot, spelt Lonow 1516, Lunna 1749.
Penberthy, Penberth	From pen-perthy: end of bushes. Place names Penberth, St. Buryan; Penperth, St. Just in Roseland. Found in West Cornwall.
Pencavel	Uncertain derivation. Possibly from pen-kevil: horse head, or pen-kevelek, woodcock's head. Parish name St. Michael Penkevil.
Pendarves, Pendarvis	From pen-derow or pen-dar: end of oak trees. Place name Pendarves, Camborne.
Pender, Penter, Paynter	From pen-dyr: end of land. Name found in West Cornwall, still close to Land's End.
Pendray, Pendry	From pen-dre: end of homestead, or chief or upper homestead. Place name, Pendrea, St. Buryan and Gulval.
Penellum	From pen-ylyn: clean or bright head. Place name Penalym, Jacobstow.
Penfound	Possibly from pen-fawen: end of beech trees. Place name Penfound, Otterham.
Pengelly, Pengilly	From pen-kelly: end or head of copse or grove. Place name Pengelly in 13 parishes. Name found throughout Cornwall.
Penglaze	From pen-glas: green, grey head or top (hill). Place name Penglaze, Lansallos and St. Allen.

Penhale, Penhaul	From pen-hal: end, or top of moor. Place name in 23 parishes. Found in Mid-West & N. Cornwall.
Penhaligon	From pen-helygen: end of willow tree. Place name Penhaligon, Bodmin. Found in Mid Cornwall.
Penhallow	From pen-hallow: end of moors or downs.
Penhallurick, Penlerick	Place name Penhalurick, Stithians, from pen-hallurek: top of cultivated ground on moor. Found in Mid Cornwall.
Penhorwood	Possibly from pen-horth- (wood): end of ram's wood. Name first appeared in Kilkhampton Parish Register 1620.
Penna, Penney	From an-penna: chiefest, or from pennow: tops, heads. Found in Mid and North Cornwall.
Penneck	From pen-knegh: top of the hillock Place name Penknight, Lostwithiel, spelt Penknek 1269.
Pennell	Still extant. From Pen +?: head or chief?
Penprase, Penpraze	From pen-pras: end of meadow. Place name Penprase, Illogan, Praze, Crowan and St. Erth. Found in Mid-West Cornwall.
Penrice	From pen-res: end of ford. Place name Penrice, St. Austell.
Penrose	From pen-ros: end or top of heath, moor. Place name found in 10 parishes. Found in Mid and West Cornwall.
Pentecost	Chirgwin suggests: pen-ty-cos: chief house in the wood.
Pentreath	From pen-treth: top or end of beach. Place name Pentreath, Breage. Found in West Cornwall.
Penver	From pen-(m)vur: big hill-top.
Penwarden, Penwarne	From pen-gwernen: end of alder trees. Place name Penwarne, in Mawnan, Cuby & Mevagissey. Found in Mid, SE. and North Cornwall.
Pepper	Possibly from peber: baker.

Permewan	From parish name St. Mewan, possibly as porth – mewan: the cove or beach St. Mewan.
Perrin, Perring, Perren	From St Perran patron saint of tin miners.
Perrow	Possibly from Porthow: beaches, cove. Place name ? Polperro, Talland. Alternative derivation: from perrow: cauldrons, crocks.
Petherick, Pedrick, Pethick	Diminutive of Petroc, father of Cornish saints. Parish name Little Petherick. Found in Mid and North Cornwall.
Pethybridge	Hybrid, derived from Petherick (Petroc). Found in Mid Cornwall.
Pezzack	Breakaway from place name Carne Pessack, St. Keverne (Carpesak, 1300), Car-pesak, decayed fort. Jenner suggests (ma)p ysak-son of Isaac.
Pill	Possibly from pyl: hillock or pile. Place name Pill, Lanlivery spelt Lapyle 1379. Found in Mid and Mid West Cornwall.
Pinnick	From pen ewyk: headland frequented by deer. Place name Pinnick, Fowey, spelt Penuwyk, 1390.
Pinnock, Pennock	From parish name St. Pinnock.
Pleming	From plu men: parish (boundary) stone.
Polglaze	From pol-glas green or blue pool Found in Far West Cornwall. Place name in 12 parishes.
Polgrean, Polgreen	From pol growyn: pool with gravel or grit – gravel pit, or pol-grun: dammed-up pond. Place name Polgrean in Cury, St Wenn & Mawgan in Pydar.
Polkinghorne, Polkinhorn	From pol -Kynhorn: pool of Kynhorn. (iron-chief). Place name Polkinghorne Gwinear. Widely distributed.
Pollak, Pollok, Pollock	If Cornish, from pol-lok: pool by monastic cell.
Pollard	From pol: pool +?. Place name Pollard, near Helston.
Polmear, Pelmear	From pol-mur: big pool. See Pelmear.
Polsue	From pol-(d)su: dark, black pool. Place name Polsue, in St. Ewe, Cuby, St. Erme and Philleigh. Found in West Cornwall.

Polwhele	From either pol (g)wel: pool in open field or pol – whyl: pool of beetles. Place name Polwhele, St. Clement and Gwinear.
Polwin	From pol-wyn: fair or white pool. Place name Polwin, Cury spelt Penhalwen 1287, hence end of the white moor. Found in Falmouth.
Pool, Poole, Pooley	Probably from pol: pool.
Pope	Widely found in Kernow. In 13th and 14th cents shown as popa: Puffin?
Powell	From Map-Howel: son of Howel (personal name). Found Mid, S. E. & North Cornwall.
Praed	From pras: meadow.
Preece, Price, Pryce	From (Ma)p Res: son of Rees (from res: ford).
Prideaux	Possibly from pry-tyas: clay covered, or perhaps from Norman French. Place name Prideaux, Luxulyan, spelt Prydias 1249. Found in S. E. & North Cornwall.
Prisk	From prysk: bushes, brushwood. Place name Prisk, Mullion. Found in Mid West Cornwall.
Prout	From nickname prowt: proud, puffed-up.
Prowse, Prouse	From map-ros: son of heath. Found throughout Cornwall.
Pryor	From pry: clay? Otherwise from Eng. Eccles:prior.
Prynne, Prinn	From map-ryn: son of hillside or slope, or son of Rynne (personal name). Found in Mid, S. E. & North Cornwall.
Quick	From gwyk: wood or village. Place names Polquick, St. Clement; Gweek, Constantine. Found in Far West Cornwall.
Quintrell	Probably personal name or from quin (goon)-Terrel, Terrel's down.
Rawe, Row, Rowe	Cornish form of Ralph or Radulphus.
Rees, Reece, Rhys, Rice	From res: ford. Place name Rice, Gorran (spelt Rys 1327). Found throughout Cornwall.

Repper, Ripper	From place names Bareppa, Mawnan; Berepper, Gunwalloe and Kenwyn; Barripper, Camborne – derived from French beau-repere, beautiful retreat. Found in Mid & Mid West Cornwall.
Rescorla, Roscorla, Scholler	From ros-corlan: heath of sheepfold or res - corlan: ford of sheepfold. Place name Rescorla, St. Austell & St. Ewe (Reskorlan 1311).
Reseigh	From res-segh: dry ford. Place name Rissick, St. Buryan (Ressegh 1296). Found in far in West Cornwall.
Reskelly, Roskelly	From res (ford) or ros (heath) and kelly: by the grove or copse.
Restarick	From ros-dowrak: heath (or res, ford) of watery place.
Retallack, Retallick	From res-talek: ford at base of short, steep slope. Place names Retallack, St. Columb Major and St. Hilary and Retallick, Constantine.
Roach, Roche	From parish name Roche, derived from French roche, rock. Found Mid and West Cornwall.
Rodda	Probably personal name.
Roose, Rose, Ruse	From ros: heath, promontory. Place names Rose, Perranzabubloe, Roose, Laneast, Otterham, Minster. Found S. E. & North Cornwall.
Roscarrock	From ros-carrek: rocky heath or promontory.
Roscrow, Roskrow	From ros-crow: heath with a hut. Place name Roskrow, St. Gluvias.
Rosdew	From ros-du: dark, black heath.
Rosemayle	From ros-Mael: Mael's heath. See Maile.
Rosemergy, Rosemurgy	From ros-mergh-(dy): stable (lit. horse-house) on heath or moor. Place name Rosemurgey, Morvah.
Rosevear	From ros vur: big heath or moor. Place name Rosevear, St. Austell and Mawgan in Meneage. Found mostly in Mid Cornwall.
Rosewall	From res-(g)wal: ford by the rampart or wall. Place name Rosewall, Towednack (Ryswall 1327). Found in Far West Cornwall.

Rosewarne	From ros-(g)wern: heath with alders. Place name Rosewarne, Camborne (Roswern 1380). Found in West Cornwall.
Roskelly, Roskilly	From res (ford) or ros (heath)-kelly: by the grove or copse. Place name Roskilly, St. Keverne. Found in Mid Cornwall.
Roskruge	From ros-cruk: heath of the barrow or mound. Place name Roskruge, St. Anthony in Meneage. Found in Mid West Cornwall.
Ross	From ros: heath or promomtory. Ross marriages recorded in 7 parishes from 1600-1812.
Rouse, Rowse, Rows	From ros: heath or promontory. Place name Rouse, Pillaton; Roose, Laneast and Treneglos. Widely spread throughout Cornwall.
Rowell, Rule	Personal name Ryual, (powerful king). Cornish word rewl: direction, control, rule. Place names Trerule, St. Germans (Trerewal 1310): Reawla, Gwinear. Found in Mid-West, Mid and SE. Cornwall.
Ryall	See above. Found in SE. Cornwall.
Sallos, Sallis, Sallows	Breakaway from parish name Lansallos-lan-Salwys.
Sandry, Saundry	From sentry: sanctuary, glebe. Found in Mid and North Cornwall.
Sanders, Saunders	Cornish form of Alexander. Found Mid and SE. Cornwall.
Sara	Cornish surname for at least 7 centuries. Derivation obscure. Found in Mid and West Cornwall. Chirgwin suggests from ser: wood-worker, artificer.
Sawle, Sowell	Probably personal name Sawel. Place names Tresawle, Colan, Probus, St. Columb Major (spelt Tresawel 1338). Found Mid and West Cornwall.
Sayce	From Saws: Saxon (English). Place names Carsize, Crowan; Trezaise, Roche.
Scaddan	Probably breakaway from Rosecaddon, Manaccan (spelt Roskadon 1300 – hence heath of Cadon).

Scawn, Scown	From scawen: elder-tree. Place name Penscawn, St. Enoder. See Boscawen.
Scobey	Possibly form of Sobey, or vice versa.
Scoble, Scobel	Derivation uncertain, possibly from epscop: bishop, or eboll: colt. Place name Trescobeas, Budock, spelt Treskybaes 1284; Trezebal, Manaccan spelt Tresebel, 1284.
Scorce	Possibly a breakaway from place name Roskors, St. Enoder – ros cors: heath with fen or bog.
Scott	From Scotti: bands of Adventurers. Name found widely in Cornwall from 14th century.
Scrase	Possibly from place names Scraesdon, Antony and Scrawsdon, St. Ive. Scraw: black-headed gull.
Sellick	Possibly from personal name Salac.
Sholl	Derivation obscure, possibly of Hugenot origin. Flourished in 17th-19th Cents.
Shugg, Chugg	From chogha: chough or jackdaw. Found in East and West Cornwall.
Skewes	From skewys: sheltered (place). Place names Skewes, Cury and Crowan; Treskewes, Stithians; Skewyt, St. Wenn. Found in West Cornwall.
Sloggett	Breakaway from place name Tresloggett, St. Mabyn (Tresloget 1331). Found in North and East Cornwall.
Snell	From snel: quick, active, speedy.
Soady, Sawdey,	Possibly from saw-dy: safe, well (built) house. Found Mid and SE. Cornwall.
Sobey	Name recorded 113 times in 1963 registers. See Scobey.
Sowden, Sowdon	From souder-den: soldier-man. Found in Mid West, SE. and North Cornwall.
Spargo	From place name Spargo, Mabe (spelt Spergour 1318 – spern-cor: corner with thorns). Found in Mid and Mid West Cornwall.

Sparnon	From spernen: thorn bush. Place name Sparnon, Breage, Budock, Redruth, St. Buryan.
Spettigue	Breakaway from place name Spettigue, Altarnun (spelt Rospethigou 1332, Trespethegou 1401), ros – Pethick: heath of Pethick (Patrick).
Stevens	Cornish form of Stephen – a deeply Celtic name used from 5th century onwards. Found chiefly in Far West and SE. Cornwall.
Sweet	Place name Tresweeta, St. Stephen in Brannel; Sweet's House, Lanlivery, mentioned in 1302. Found in East and North Cornwall.
Tallack	From talek: big-browed (nickname). Found in Mid West and Mid Cornwall.
Talling, Tallon	Parish name Talland. Place name Nanstallon, Bodmin – nans Talon: Talon's valley. Talon is old Cornish personal name in Bodmin Gospels 970. Found in East Cornwall.
Tangye	Breton name Tanguy – Cornish tansys: bonfire, or tangy: fire dog. Found in Parish Registers from 1606. Now in Mid and Mid West Cornwall.
Taskis	From tal-skes: sheltered front (hillside). Place name Taskus, Gwinear (Talscus 1317).
Teague, Teagle	From tek: fair, beautiful. Place names Nanteague, St.Allen; Rosteague, Gerrans.
Terrill, Terrell	Personal name Terril, occurs in 1327 LSR. See Botterell. Found in Mid West Cornwall.
Thake	Breakaway from place name Trethake, St. Cleer, Lanteglos by Fowey and Veryan. Tre- Daec: homestead of Daec derivative or diminutive of da: good.
Thew	From du: dark. Place name Carthew, St. Issey and Wendron.
Thorne	Possibly from thron: nose or point of land. Place name Eathorne, Mabe (Ethron, 1417). Found in West and North Cornwall.
Thow	From du: dark. Recorded since 1327 See Thew.

Tiddy	Place name River Tiddy, SE. Cornwall. Possibly derived from tyd: tide of sea. Found in Mid and West Cornwall.
Tilly, Tilley	Possibly from tylly: deserve, pay, be worth. Place name Pentille, St. Mellion.
Tink, Tynk	From tynk: finch. Found in East Cornwall.
Tinney	Possibly from place names St. Tinney, Otterham, and Bartinney, St. Just in Penwith. Found in Mid and North Cornwall.
Tippett	Cornish form of Thibaud (Theobald).
Tollick	From tollek: place with holes or pits.
Toman	Probably from tomen: earth bank, dyke.
Tossell	From parish name St. Austell. Found in East Cornwall.
Trahair	From tregher: tailor, cutter. Found in Far West.
Trannack	From tre-Vranoc: homestead of Branoc (Personal name). Place names Trannack, Madron and Sancreed (spelt Trevanek, 1334).
Trathen	From trethen: small sandy patch. Found in Far West Cornwall.
Trays, Treaise, Trease	From Tre-Res: homestead by the ford. Place name Treaise, Cury and St. Just in Penwith.
Trebarthen	Probably from tre-perthy: homestead with bushes. Place name Trebartha, North Hill.
Trebell	From tre-bell: distant homestead. Place name Trebell, Lanivet. Found in Truro area.
Trebilcock	Possibly from tre-pyl-cok: homestead with cuckoo-haunted hillock? or home-stead of Pilcok, (red Bill) personal name. Place name Trebilcock, Roche (Trebiloc 1302). Found in Mid, North and SE. Cornwall.
Tredinnick	From tre-redenek: homestead in fern-brake, or tre –dynek: homestead by the little fort. Place name in 14 parishes. Found in Mid-West and S. E Cornwall.

Tredrea, Tredray	From place name Tredrea, St. Erth (spelt Tredreu 1301). Derivation obscure. Found in West Cornwall.
Tredwen	Possibly from place name Tredwen, Davidstow, spelt Riguen in Domesday Book, res- (g)wyn: fair ford.
Treen	From tre-ryn: homestead on the hillside or tre-dyn: homestead of hill fort. Place names Treen, St. Levan and Zennor (spelt Trethyn 1314 tre-dyn).
Treffry	Possibly from tre- (b)vre: homestead on hill. Place names Treffry, Lanhydrock; Merther, St. Gluvias.
Trefusis	Place name Trefusis, Mylor, where family reside. Spelt Trefuses in 12th cent. Derivation unknown.
Tregale	From tre-an-Galla, homestead of the Gaul. Place name Trengale, St. Cleer (Trengalla 1334).
Treganowan	Possibly from tre-ganow: homestead at mouth or hollow, or from tre -gonyow: homestead on the downs. Place name Treganun, Lanlivery (spelt Tregunnou 1331). Found in Truro area.
Tregarthen	From tre-cardhen: homestead with thicket or brake. Place name Tregarthen, Ludgvan. Found in West Cornwall.
Tregaskes, Tregaskis	From tre-goskes: homestead in a shady sheltered place. Found in Mid Cornwall.
Tregea, Tregay	From tre-ke: homestead with hedge bank. Place name Tregea, Illogan.
Tregeagle, Tregagle	From tre-cagal: homestead of dunghill. Place name Tregeagle, Probus.
Tregear	From tre-ger: homestead by fort. Place name Tregear occurs in 8 parishes. Found in Far West.
Tregellas, Tregelles	Possibly from tre-(k)gellys: the lost or hidden homestead, or homestead of Celestis. Place names Tregelles, St. Kew, Tregillis, S.Petherwin; Tregellas, Ludgvan; Tregellast, St. Keverne.
Tregembo	From tre-(k)gemper: homestead where streams meet. Place name Tregembo St. Hilary.

Tregenna, Tregunna	From tre-gonyow: homestead on downs, or from tre-Cenue (personal name). Place names Tregenna and Tregunna in many parishes.
Tregenza	From tre-kensa: first or foremost homestead. Found in Far and Mid West and Mid Cornwall.
Tregidgo, Tregidga	Possibly from tre-ky-chyow: homestead with kennels (dog-houses) or from tre-crys: shaky (boggy) homestead. Place name Tregidga Creed (spelt Tregrisiou 1332). Found in Mid Cornwall.
Tregilgas	From tre- and personal name Gilgis. Place name Tregilgas, St. Teath (spelt Tregilgis 1579).
Treglown, Tregloan	Possibly from tre-ke-loghyn: homestead with hedge by the little lake or inlet. Place name Treglohan, St. Keverne (spelt Tregeloghan 1270). Found in West and North Cornwall.
Tregoning	From tre-ke-onnen: homestead with hedge of ash trees or tre-Conan: Conan's homestead. Place name in 8 parishes. Found in West Cornwall.
Tregurtha	Derivation uncertain, possibly from tre-kerghen: homestead of oats. Place name Tregurtha, St. Hilary. Found in Far West Cornwall.
Trehane	Possibly from tre-Iahan: John's homestead. Place name Trehane in Davidstow, Trevalga, Probus, Cury (all with early spellings Treyahan).
Trehearne	From tre-hem: homestead where iron is. Compare Trestain.
Trelawney, Trelawny	Possibly from tre-lonow: homestead of groves. Place name Trelawney, Altarnun; Trelawne, Pelynt.
Trelease	From tre-lys: homestead of or by the court or hall. Place name Trelease, St. Keverne and Kea. Found in Mid West Cornwall.
Treleaven, Treleven, Treliving	From tre-leven: level homestead, or homestead of Leven (personal name). Place name Treleaven, Mevagissey. Found in Mid and North Cornwall.
Treloar	From tre-lowarth: homestead with garden. Place name Treloar, Wendron. Found in West and Mid Cornwall.

Tremaine, Tremayne	From tre-meyn: homestead of stones. Parish name Tremaine. Place names Tremayne and Tremain in 5 parishes. Found in Mid West and North Cornwall.
Trembath, Tenbath	From tre-an-bagh: homestead in the nook or corner. Place name Trembath, Madron (spelt Trenbagh 1327). Wide-spread.
Trembeth	From tre-an-beth: homestead by the grave. Found in Mid Cornwall.
Tremberth, Trenberth	From tre-an-berth: homestead by the bush. Found in Mid and West Cornwall.
Tremearne	Possibly from tre- mernans: homestead of death. Place name Tremearne, Madron, spelt Tremern 1445.
Tremeer	From tre-mur: big homestead. Place name Tremeer in 5 parishes.
Tremelling	From tre-melyn: homestead of mill. Place name Tremelling, St. Erth. Found in Mid-West Cornwall.
Tremenheere	From tre-men-hyr: homestead by long-stone (menhir).
Tremethick	From tre-medhek: homestead of doctor. Place name Tremethick, Madron.
Tremewan	From tre-Mewan: homestead of Mewan (personal name cf. St. Mewan).
Trenance	From tre-nans: homestead in valley. Place name in 6 parishes.
Trenary, Trenerry	From tre(v)-an-erow: homestead in the field. Place name Trenerry, St. Allen (spelt Trevenery 1327). Found in Mid Cornwall.
Trenear, Treneer	From tre-an-yer: homestead of the hens -? a poultry farm. Place name Trenear, Wendron, Treneer, Madron (spelt Trenyer 1280).
Trengove	From tre-an-gof: homestead of the smith. Place name Trengove, Illogan.
Trengrouse	From tre-an-grows: homestead by the cross.
Trenhaile	From tre-an-hal: homestead on the down or moor. Place name Trenhale, Newlyn East.

Trenouth, Trenoweth	From tre-noweth: new homestead. Place name Trenouth, St. Ervan and Tintagel; Trenoweth, Probus; Trenowth, St. Cleer and St. Columb Major. Found in SE. & N. Cornwall.
Trenowden, Renowden	Cornish form of Renaud or Reginald, hence tre Renowden. Renowden's homestead.
Trenwith	From tre-Iunwith: Iunwith's homestead. Place name Trenwith, St. Ives, spelt Treyunwith 1391.
Trepress	From tre-pras: homestead in meadow. See also Press.
Trerise	From tre-res: homestead by ford. Place name Trerice, St. Dennis, St. Allen, Crowan St. Breock, Ruan Major. Found West Cornwall.
Tresawna	From tre-saunyow: homestead by deep clefts in cliffs. See Tresawne, Trezona.
Tresawne, Trezona	Possibly from tre-saunyow: homestead by clefts in cliff. Place name Tresawna, St. Enoder, spelt Tresagnou, 1290.
Trescothick	From tre-scawek: homestead of elder grove. Place name Trescowthick, Newlyn East. Found in Mid and Mid-West Cornwall.
Treseder, Tresidder	From tre-Seder: Seder's homestead. Place name Tresidder, Constantine and St. Buryan (spelt Treseder 1327).
Tresise, Trezise	From tre-Saws: homestead of the Saxon, Englishman. Place name Trezise, St. Martin in Meneage, Tresayes, Roche. Found in West Cornwall.
Trestain	From tre-sten: homestead at tin place. Place name Trestain, Ruanlanihorne.
Trestrail	From tre-strayl: homestead of mat or carpet (maker). Place name Trestrail, Probus, spelt Trestrael 1278.
Trethake	From tre-(D)thaoc: Daoc's homestead. Place name Trethake, St. Cleer and Lanteglos by Fowey; Tretheake, Veryan; Tredegue, Gwennap.
Trethewey	From tre-(D)thewi: homestead of David (Dewi) Place name in many parishes, spelt Tredewi 13th cent.

Trethowan	From tre-(D)thewin: homestead of Dewin. Place name Trethowan, Constantine, spelt Trevewen 1295. Found in Mid West Cornwall.
Trevail, Treveal	From tre-(M)vael: homestead of Mael. Place name Treveal, Zennor, Ladock, Cubert.
Trevain, Trevains	Possibly from tre vyhan: little homestead.
Trevan	Possibly from tal-ban: high hillside. Place name Trevan, Probus, spelt Talfan 1361.
Trevanion	From trev-Enyon: homestead of Enyon. Place names Trevanion, St. Breock & St. Mewan (spelt Trevenyon 1326).
Trevartha	From trev-Affa: Affa's homestead. Place name Trevartha, Menheniot (Trevaffa 1345).
Trevarthen, Trevarton Treverton	From trev-Arthien: Arthien's homestead. Place names Trevarthian, St. Hilary and Newlyn East, Trevathen, St. Kew (Trevarthean 1237).
Trevaskis	From tre-(M)valscuet: Maelscuet's homestead. Place name Trevaskis, Gwinear; Trevascus, Gorran, both with old spellings Trevalscoys. Found in West Cornwall.
Trevean	From tre-vyhan: little homestead.
Trevellick	Possibly from trev – Elec: Elec's homestead or tre-(m)velynyk: homestead by the little mill.
Trevelyan, Trevillion	From tre – (M)vilian: Milian's homestead. Place name Trevelyan, St. Veep; Trelean, St. Erth and St. Teath (with early spelling Trevelyan). Found in Far West Cornwall.
Trevena, Trevenna	From tre-(m)veneth: homestead on hill, or tre-(m)vun: homestead with minerals. Place names Trevena, Breage (Trevuns 1436) and Trevena, Tintagel (Trewarvene 1259). Found in Mid West Cornwall.
Trevenen	From tre-(m)veyn wyn: homestead of white stones, or tre-venen: homestead of the woman. Place name Trevennen, Wendron (Trevenwyn 1301) and Gorran (Trevenyen 1393). Found in Far West Cornwall. Chirgwin suggests from trev-Enyon: Enyon's homestead. Cf. Trevanion.

Trevethan	From tre-(b)vuthyn: homestead in a meadow. Place name Trevethan, St. Eval, Budock, Gwennap.
Trevethick, Trevithick	From tre- (B)vudic: Budic's homestead. Place name Trevithick in St. Columb Major, St. Columb Minor, Perranzabubloe, St. Ewe & St. Teath. Found in West Cornwall.
Trevisa	From trev-ysa: lowest homestead. Place names Trevisa, Trevegia.
Trevivian	From tre-Vyvyan: Vyvyan's homestead. Place name Trevivian, Davidstowe.
Trevor	From tre-(M)vor: Mor's homestead. Mor is a personal name found in Bodmin Gospels. Place name Trevor, St. Buryan.
Trevorrow, Treverrow, Trevarrow	From tre-Vorva: Vorva's homestead, or from treforthow: homestead by the tracks. Place name Trevorrow, Ludgvan (Treworvou 1299).
Trew, True	Obscure. Place names Trew, Breage and Tresmeer and Treau, St. Buryan, all have variety of early spellings and perhaps no common origin.
Trewartha	From tre-wartha: upper homestead. Place name Trewartha, St. Agnes.
Trewavas	From tre-(g)wavas: winter homestead. Place name Trewavas, Breage and Wendron.
Treweek	From tre-(g)wyk: homestead at or in wood or village. Place name Treweeg, Stithians.
Trewen	From tre-(g)wyn: white or fair homestead. Parish name Trewen. Place name Trewen in St. Tudy, Lanreath, Budock.
Trewern, Trewren	From tre-(g)wern: homestead by marsh or swamp. Place name Trewern, Madron.
Trewhella	Possibly from tre-ughella: highest homestead. Found in West Cornwall and Mid Cornwall. Place names Trewhella, St. Hilary; Trewhela, St. Enoder.
Trewin	From tre-(g)wyn: fair or white homestead. Place name Trewin, Sheviock.

Trewolla	Possibly from tre-(g)wallow: homestead by ramparts. Place name Trewoll, Gorran and Constantine.
Treworgie	Probably from tre- and personal name, as Gwrgy. Place name Trewirgie, Redruth.
Triggs	From Trigg, name of ancient Hundred, but now found in Far West.
Triniman	Possibly from tre-nawmen: homestead by the stone circle (lit. 'nine stones') Found in Mid West Cornwall.
Trinick, Trinnick	Possibly as Trannack; tre-(B)vranoc homestead of Branoc (personal name).
Tripconey	If from place name Trekenning, St. Columb Major (Tripeconnynge 1594) second element may come from root conyn: rabbit. Found in Far West Cornwall.
Tripp	Derivation uncertain, unless from Welsh tripio, to trip.
Troon	From tre-wun: homestead on the dowr. Place name Troon, Breage, Camborne; Phillack; Trewoon, St. Austell.
Trounson	From tre-rounsyn: homestead of donkey or nag. Found in Far West Cornwall.
Trudgian, Trudgen, Trudgeon, Tregian	Possibly from tre- cun: homestead dogs. Name found as Tregyan 1257. Alternative derivation: tre-ojyon: homestead of oxen. Place name Tregian, St. Ewe. Found in Mid Cornwall.
Truran, Truan	From tre-(g)wern: homestead by marsh or swamp. See Trewern, of which variant.
Truscott	Possibly from dres-cos: across the wood. Place name Truscott, St. Stephens by Launceston. Found in Mid Cornwall.
Trussell	From tre-(G)wystyl: Gwystyl's homestead. Place name Trussel, Tremaine & St. Keyne.
Trythall	Place name Trythall, Gulval, spelt Trewrethal 1297, Trevrethial 1324, hence probably from tre- and personal name. Found in West Cornwall.
Tudor	Personal name – Cornish King Teudar. Place names, Lestowder, St. Keverne; Bosteeda, Crowan.

Turk	If Cornish, from towarghek: peaty (land).
Tyack	From tyak: farmer, peasant. Found west of Truro.
Tyzzer	Variant of personal name Teudar. See Tudor.
Udy	From parish name St. Tudy, name of a Breton saint. Found Mid, N. & S. E. Cornwall.
Ugalde	From ughel-dyr: high land, upland. Found only in Liskeard area.
Uglow	Possibly from ughella: higher, hence yeomen or upper people, or from ughlogh, upper inlet. Found in S. E. & North Cornwall.
Uren	From gwern: swamp or marsh, breakaway from place name Trewern, Madron (Trewruen 1302). Chirgwin suggests from personal name Ewryn. 4 Bretons named Uren appear in 1523 LSR for Gwennap parish.
Ursell	From ysella: lowness, hence possibly 'down the hill'.
Ustick	Personal name, or Ust-yk: St. Just people.
Vague, Vage	Possibly a breakaway from place name Trevague, Altarnun (Trevagau, Domesday Book) tre-(m)vage homestead for rearing Or raising. Found in SE. and Mid Cornwall.
Varcoe, Vercoe, Varker	Probably Mark's children. Found in Mid Cornwall.
Vaughan, Vian, Vyan, Vine	From vyhan: little, in tre-vyhan, little homestead.
Veal, Veale, Vail	From personal name Mael or Myghal. Place names Treveal, Zennor & Cubert; Busveal, Gwennap.
Vear	Breakaway from place name as Rosevear in St. Austell and Mawgan in Meneage or Carvear, St. Blazey, ros-vur: great heath, car-vur: great camp.
Vellacott	Possibly from melyn-cot: mill wood, or if second element is English mill cottage.
Vellam	From Melyn: mill.
Vellanoweth	From (m)velyn-noweth: new mill. Place name Vellanoweth, Ludgvan and St. Agnes; Vellanouth, Constantine.

Venner	From meneth: hill. Place name Colvenner, Wendron (spelt Colveneth 1461).
Venning	Probably breakaway from place name Trevennen, Wendron & Gorran (both with old spellings tre-ven-wyn: homestead of white stone).
Venton	From fenten: spring, fountain. Place name Venton North Tamerton, Menheniot & St. Germans. Found in Mid Cornwall.
Verran, Verrin	Probably derived from ver: short, hence a short man. Place names Buscaverran, Crowan: Ponsaverran, Constantine. Found in Mid & SE. Cornwall.
Vial	Variant of Veal, q.v.
Viant, Vian	Possibly a form of Vaughan, or derived from (b)vyhan: small.
Vickery	If Cornish, possibly from vycarjy: vicarage (servant). Found in S. E. & North Cornwall.
Vigus, Vigars	Possibly from var-cos: top of wood. Place name Busvargus, St. Just in Penwith (Bosvargoes 1302)
Vingoe	Possibly a breakaway from place name Trevingey St. Ives, derivation obscure. Found only in West Cornwall. Alternative derivation, from (m)ven-ky: stone dog. Place name: Trevingey, Redruth.
Vinson	Possibly from fenten: spring, fountain. Place name Trevenson, Illogan (Trefensin 1340).
Visick	Possibly from place name Trevisick – trev-ysak: homestead with cornfield. Place names Trevisick in Poundstock, Blisland, St. Agnes, St. Austell all with spelling Trevisek 1274, Trevysack 1327. Found in Mid and S. E. Cornwall.
Vivian, Vyvyan	Personal name with documented history of at least 7 centuries in Cornwall, now widely distributed throughout the land. Place name Trevivian, Davidstowe.
Vosper	From fos-por: pasture by ditch or rampart. Place name Trevosper, S. Petherwin (spelt Trevospor 1210). Found in SE. & North Cornwall.

Voss, Vos ,Vose	From fos: ditch or rampart. Place name Vose, St. Ewe.
Wall	From (g)wal: wall or rampart. Place name Wall, Gwinear. Found in Far West & Mid Cornwall.
Wallace, Wallis	Possibly from Saxon Weales: strangers, applied to native Britons, or from a-woles: below (down along). Found in West Cornwall.
Walsh, Welch, Welsh	From Saxon Wealas: strangers, applied to native Britons, as Wallace above.
Warne, Wearne	From (g)wern: swamp or alders. Place names Rosewarne, Camborne (Roswern 1380), Penwarne, Mawnan, Cuby & Mevagissey (Penwern 1327). Found in Far West, Mid and S. E. Cornwall.
Warren	As Warne – from (g)wern: alder grove. Found West, SE. & North Cornwall.
Warrick	Probably personal name Worek. Place names Treworrick, St. Cleer & St. Ewe (Treworek 1339) Rosewarrick, Lanivet (Rosworok 1250). Found in Mid & SE Cornwall.
Weary, Wherry, Werry	Possibly from personal name Gweri. Place name Trewerry, Newlyn East (Treweri 1201). Found in Mid and SE Cornwall.
Week, Weeks	From gwyk: wood or village. Place name Treweeg, Stithians (Trewyk 1326).
Weighell	Possibly from whegoll: dearest.
Werring, Wearing, Werren	Possibly from personal name Weryn. Parish name Werrington. Found in SE Cornwall.
Wevell, Wivell	From name of SE Cornwall Hundred -Wivelshire. Still found in SE Cornwall.
Wheal, Whale, Whell	From whel: mine working. Place name Trenwheal, Breage. Found in SE. Cornwall.
Whear, Wheare, Ware	Possibly from either gwer: green or whar: gentle, humble.
Wickett	Derivation obscure. Place name Wickett, Newlyn East. Found in Mid and North Cornwall.

Widdon	Probably from gwyn: fair. Place name Trewidden Madron (Trewen 1300).
Wilce, Willis, Willes	Possibly from personal name Welet (recorded in Bodmin Manumissions). Place name Trewillis, St. Keverne (Trewelles 1300).
Windle, Wintle	From gwennol: swallow. Place names Tregwindle, St. Neot (Tregwennell 1516) Tregwindles, St. Breock (Tregwynnell 1280).
Windsor, Winsor, Winser	Recorded in Cornwall from 1327 onwards, but origin obscure. Place name Windsor, Mawgan in Meneage.
Winn, Wynne	From gwyn: fair, white. Found in West and North Cornwall.
Winnen	Possibly from wynnen: weeds. Name recorded in Cornwall as far back as 1327. Place name Carwynnen, Crowan.
Withiel	From parish name Withiel, possibly personal name Widiel.
Woon	From gun: downland. Place name Woon, Roche; Trewoon in St. Mewan and Budock.
Worden	Possibly from war-dyn: on the hill fort, or from gwern: marsh, swamp, as in Warne. Found in SE. & North Cornwall.
Wren	Varient of Uren, q.v. gwern: swamp, marsh.
Youren	See Uren, probably from gwern: marsh, swamp.

Surnames no longer in use in Cornwall

Amongst the Cornish Celtic surnames appearing in Cornish Parish Registers in the seventeenth century, appeared the following names which had disappeared by the mid-20th century. Some of them may still be borne by descendants of Cornish people overseas.

Angarrack	Halvossa	Reeth
Angollan	Hendry	Reskeen
Angrouse	Kerne	Reskymer
Annis	Kerrow	Roscarrock
Anstey	Killiow	Rosevean
Besawsacke	Lanarth	Trebethick
Binner	Lancollas	Tregarrick
Busvargus	Penalynsy	Treleigh
Cant	Pengwedna	Trenarwyn
Carminow	Pengwidden	Trenow
Carthewy	Penhallow	Trevossow
Curnock	Penhellick	Trewan
Currow	Penpryne	Trewinnard
Erisey	Poldavy	Vanson
Greep	Polgray	

MANUMISSIONS IN THE BODMIN GOSPELS

The Bodmin, or St Petrock's Gospels (Add. Ms. 9381 British Museum) contain, at the beginning and end, manumissions of serfs, that is, notices of the freeing of serfs or slaves at the altar of St. Petrock in Bodmin in the presence of witnesses. From these about two hundred Cornish words may be gathered. Of the manumitters only five have Cornish names but amongst the manumitted slaves there are about 98 Cornish names, and some 50 Cornish witnesses. The following names form elements in Cornish surnames:

Byrsige	- hence the name Bersey and place name Trebursye
Custentin	- hence Cossentine and Constantine
Grifiud	- hence Griffiths, Griffin
Keth	- meaning serf, bondman or slave – hence Keat, Buckett
Loi	- hence Loy
Lwchi	- hence Lukey and place name Trelucky
Milian	- hence Treelyan, Trevillion
Mor	- hence Trevor
Noy	- hence surname Noy
Riol, Ryel	- hence Ryall
Talan	- hence Talling and place names Talland, Nanstallon
Welet	- hence Willis, Wilce
Wurci	- hence Treworgey, Trewirgie

BIBLIOGRAPHY

BICE Christopher.	Names for the Cornish (Dyllansow Truran1970).
BLEWETT R.R.	Celtic Surnames in Cornwall. (Ms. 1970 2 vols unpublished). Atlas of Surname Distribution in Cornwall 1953. (4 vols., with maps, unpublished). The Last Onslaught of the Saxons in West Cornwall: A Study in Depth of the Cornish Celtic Surnames Curnow and Harvey. (1968 – 69, unpublished).
CHIRGWIN E.	One Thousand Place Names of Cornwall (Privately published).
DEXTER T.F.G.	Cornish Names (Longman 1926).
DIXON Piers	Cornish names (1973).
GOVER J.E.	The Place names of Cornwall (4 vols. In Ms. – Royal Institution of Cornwall, Truro).
HENDERSON C.	Cornish Church Guide (1928).
HOLMES J.	1000 Cornish Place Names Explained (Dyllansow Truran 1983).
JENNER Henry	A Handbook of the Cornish Language (Nutt 1904).
NANCE R. Morton	An English-Cornish Dictionary (Federation of Old Cornwall Societies 1952). A New Cornish-English Dictionary (Federation of Old Cornwall Societies 1955). Notes on Celtic Personal Names of Cornwall (Old Cornwall, Vol. iv, Nos. 1 and 2).
PHILLIMORE and TAYLOR	Cornish Parish Registers – 30 vols. In Royal Institution of Cornwall, Truro. Index to the above by H.L. DOUCH in Royal Institution of Cornwall.
POOL P.A.S.	The Place Names of West Penwith (1973). The Field Names of West Penwith (1990).
ROWSE A.L.	The Cornish in America.
SMITH A.S.D.	Cornish Simplified (2nd edition 1955).